other books by the Trobisches:
A Baby Just Now?
Better Is Your Love Than Wine
I Loved a Girl
I Married You
The Joy of Being a Woman
Love Is a Feeling to Be Learned
Love Yourself
My Beautiful Feeling
On Our Way Rejoicing

booklets by Walter Trobisch:
Martin Luther's Quiet Time
Spiritual Dryness

Living with Unfulfilled Desires

Walter Trobisch

InterVarsity Press
Downers Grove
Illinois 60515

InterVarsity Press is the book-publishing division of Inter-Varsity Christian Fellowship, a student movement active on campus at hundreds of universities, colleges and schools of nursing. For information about local and regional activities, write IVCF, 233 Langdon St., Madison, WI 53703.

Distributed in Canada through InterVarsity Press, 1875 Leslie St., Unit 10, Don Mills, Ontario M3B 2M5, Canada.

First published under the title Mit Unerfüllten Wünschen Leben © Editions Trobisch 1978, Box 2048, D-7640 Kehl/Rhein, Germany.

The dialogue questions in the epilogue are reprinted with the permission of Marriage and Family Living magazine. © St. Meinrad Archabbey, St. Meinrad, IN 47577.

ISBN 0-87784-736-3
Library of Congress Catalog Card Number: 79-2718

Printed in the United States of America

| 18 | 17 | 16 | 15 | 14 | 13 | 12 | 11 | 10 | 9 | 8 | 7 | 6 | 5 | 4 | 3 |
| 94 | 93 | 92 | 91 | 90 | 89 | 88 | 87 | 86 | 85 | 84 | 83 | 82 | 81 | | |

Introduction

When answering mail from readers of my books, I was struck by the fact that again and again letters began—with a certain pride and satisfaction—"I am sixteen." After checking my files, I discovered that within one year, I had received nearly a hundred letters from sixteen-year-olds. Interestingly enough, there were about as many letters from boys as from girls.

It seems that this age group is in an especially difficult situation. Many have had experiences which formerly only someone age nineteen or twenty would have. These young people break loose from their families, yet at the same time are not able to stand on their own feet. They are no longer children, and they are not yet adults. It is this hanging in between which causes pain and suffering.

Their own families do not offer them the security they need. This is at least part of the reason why they hurt—and write.

Parents who read this book may be surprised that teenagers are capable of such deep thoughts and feelings, and they will be shocked by the insignificant role parents play in these letters. On the other hand, I hope they also realize how much they could help their children by a tender gesture, a loving word, verbalized praise, physical touch, time spent with them—and simple, patient listening.

It is also striking how many of these young people find support and help in a living faith and fellowship with dedicated Christians.

Again and again while answering their letters, I found myself thinking: if only Francis could read the letter from Mary she could see that she is not alone with her problem. Or if John could read the letter from Francis—and vice versa—they both could learn how the same situation looks from the perspective of the other sex.

These thoughts prompted me to collect and publish some of this correspondence, especially those letters touching on problems which are most common. All correspondents gladly and willingly gave me their permission.

This book was first published in German. But this is not the only reason I chose letters from readers living in Germany, Switzerland and Austria. I also have letters from American high-school students and know from many personal talks that they have very similar problems. Their letters, however, are not as expressive. I've often wondered but still don't know why this is so. Maybe this book will challenge American readers and encourage them to put their experiences into words. This in itself may be helpful.

An explanation of the dance course mentioned in some letters is probably in order for American readers. These courses are offered by private dance schools in Europe over a period of half a year—usually one evening per week. Almost all high schoolers attend them with their classmates and meet other students from different schools. They offer instruction in ballroom dancing as well as in manners and conduct—so that students may learn to become "gentlemen" and "young ladies." It is an opportunity for teen-agers to meet and get acquainted without pairing off or being committed. In many ways it replaces the American dating practice which often leads to a premature commitment and involvement which is for many more of a burden than a joy.

I changed, of course, the names of my correspondents, but I purposely did not change their letters. These are their original letters—unshortened and unedited. In my answers, therefore, some repetition was unavoidable. Again and again, for instance, I had to point out the importance of the boy-boy and girl-girl friendships in the development of the person, the constructive role of the feeling of shame and embarrassment, as well as the necessity to learn how to cope with tension and frustration.

Since in our time frustration is considered undesirable and therefore something to be eliminated at all cost, the chance to mature through it is overlooked. Thus, energies are lost which prove indispensable for gaining, in the deep sense of the word, the ability to love.

By the age of sixteen an art can already be learned which will prove to be an essential asset later in life—married or not. As Dietrich Bonhoeffer puts it, it is the art of how to live a fulfilled life in spite of many unfulfilled desires.

"We love each other terrifically"
1

---

*"Because we love each other so terrifically,
we wanted to sleep together.... It didn't work....
I didn't get a thing out of it."*
Doris P., age 16, high-school student

Dear Mr. Trobisch,

I've just read your book *Love Is a Feeling to Be Learned.* I liked it very much and your arguments made sense to me. There's only one thing I didn't like about it: you talked so much about Jesus, God and the Bible.

But let me first tell you about us. My boyfriend will be eighteen in June and I've just turned sixteen. We've been going steady for four and a half months. Both of us are convinced that we've never had either a girl or a boyfriend with whom we've felt so deeply understood, nor will we ever be able to be understood in this way by anyone else.

We believe that this feeling which we have for each other is love. We do not agree with you that having intercourse before marriage is not okay. On the contrary, you should know before marriage whether you fit together or not, also in the sexual realm.

I always felt, though, that a couple should go together for a long time before they sleep together. Once I felt differently, but that is past now.

Because we love each other so terrifically, we wanted to sleep together. We believe that the pill is the best means of contraception, so that is why I got a prescription for it.

Finally the moment came. We had time, were in the mood and would be undisturbed for several hours. But my boyfriend was so nervous and excited that he couldn't get an erection. He got terribly depressed, and it was only with great effort that I succeeded in cheering him up.

A week later the great moment came again. But again it didn't work. This time he didn't take it so hard. We just romped around instead and all of a sudden it worked, but it hurt so terrifically that I asked him to stop, which he did immediately. We petted and shortly before the climax I asked him to try again. We made another attempt. Again I had great pain as long as he was in me. Even afterwards a little bit. Is that normal? I didn't get a thing out of it. How come?

If you would please answer me, I would be very grateful.
Many thanks in advance,
Doris

Dear Doris,

It's good that you wrote to me. Maybe you did it out of a certain uneasy feeling that something's not quite right between you and your boyfriend.

There's a contradiction in your letter. On the one hand, you say that my arguments make sense to you. On the other hand, you act just in the opposite way. Could the negative experiences you have had not be reason enough to think about my arguments for discouraging intercourse before marriage?

You put the cart before the horse. You can only succeed in knowing each other sexually if you know each other in your hearts beforehand and trust each other completely. The physical union then becomes an expression of this mutual confidence which is, in turn, supported by the decision to stick together for life. Basically this is why you cannot try out before marriage whether you "fit together sexually"—just as you cannot try out how it feels to be dead by sleeping very deeply.

This trying out is not only impossible, it's also unnecessary. After all, the sexual organs are not made of bones, but of muscles and soft tissues which adjust to each other during the course of marriage.

What you should try out before marriage is whether you fit together in your hearts, inwardly, and this takes a lot of time—more than four and a half months. If you include the physical too soon in your relationship, the growth of this heart knowledge will be greatly hindered and sometimes even stopped.

Certainly that which you feel for each other is a type of love, but whether it's the kind of love which can bind you together for life, you cannot yet know after such a short acquaintance. I'm afraid that at your age, you cannot yet know it at all. Besides that, during the next years both of you will change decisively.

I would like to warn you and urge you not to take the pill. At your age, it can certainly cause great damage.

The pill contains artificial hormones which hinder ovulation and thereby create in your body a false state of pregnancy. This means that the normal process of development and maturing of your cycle is disturbed, and there is even a possibility that you may become infertile. Sometimes after taking the pill for a longer period of time, menstruation stops completely and then a complicated treatment will be necessary.

Did you know that several large drug firms, both in Europe and in the States, have stopped producing the pill because the lawsuits and payment of damages exceed their profits? Since these lawsuits are usually settled out of court, the public rarely hears of them. Why don't you stop abusing yourself for the benefit of the pharmaceutical industry?

Of course, what you experienced is not normal because the

physical union should bring enjoyment and not torture. However, at your age and in the situation which you described, your experience was normal to a certain degree. Many young people have similar experiences. I know many young girls who would confirm your statement: "I didn't get a thing out of it!"

There is, of course, the possibility that you experienced pain because your vagina is still very small and that, physically speaking, you have not yet fully matured. However, there might be a psychological reason: you were afraid—and, even though you might deny it, unconsciously you had a bad conscience. This could also explain why your boyfriend was unable to have an erection.

Maybe you were afraid that the pill wouldn't work 100% or that you would be caught naked. It seems strange to me that you did not mention your parents at all in your letter. What do they say? Or don't they even know about it?

I could also imagine that both of you were simply afraid of failure. When you want to try something, then success becomes very important. If you would be honest and draw the logical conclusion, you would have to say, "We do not fit together," and then break up. Since you do not even consider this possibility, you see how dishonest it is to justify premarital sex with this argument.

Maybe you can understand now why I talk about God so much in the book you read. God wants these experiences to be beautiful for us so that we can enjoy the memories of them. For this reason he has reserved this innermost communion for marriage. God does not want to deprive you of something. He wants to make you richer.

With warm greetings and the hope that you understand,
W.T.

Reflection
Doris did not understand. She did not answer at all. When I wrote to her after she had been silent for six months, she was

very surprised. "To be honest, I thought you had just given a routine answer," she said.

Evidently the fact that someone cared was a new experience for her. She answered my question about her parents with these words: "I have a very poor relationship with my parents. We only scream at each other. That's why you are the only one—and you are still the only one—who knows about Gerhard and myself in this respect. When I told my parents about the pill they did not approve of it, but they said, 'This is your business.' "

Doris's parents left their sixteen-year-old daughter alone with this important decision. She describes her dilemma: "First it didn't work at all. I was completely closed when we tried to have intercourse. Then it worked, and I took the pill for seven months. In the meantime I realized that the pill is not good for me. I gained twenty pounds, got broad hips and massive breasts which don't go with me at all.

"Then we talked about what other contraceptive we could use and decided to try the condom. We don't like it though, because it's not at all beautiful and it's so messy.

"After that experience I got the idea of having a diaphragm fitted, but my lady doctor said that the accident rate is too high, and she suggested that I use an IUD. She sent me to a gynecologist who plans to measure my uterus during the next menstruation in order to insert an IUD, if possible. The whole thing would cost me a hundred dollars. I'm just a poor high-school student, and Gerhard is an electrical apprentice.

"Some time ago my sister got an IUD inserted, but it gives her a lot of pain. I'm not sure whether I want to go through with it. If it doesn't work, the money is gone and we still don't have anything."

I am afraid Doris will never be satisfied if she continues on this road. She is indeed a poor high-school student, but in a much deeper sense than she realizes. The same is true of her boyfriend.

She does not know what to do and weighs the possibilities.

She does not even seem to consider the simplest solution, namely, that of giving up intercourse. In this case, she would have something.

Then her personality could grow. Her ability to stand up under tension would develop. If she were to give up sex, new energies would be set free which, in turn, would enable her to love in the true sense of the word.

At the moment, the two are meeting at a purely genital level and do not learn much about each other. Even if they were to marry, which is quite unlikely, their marriage would probably become empty and insipid. After the sexual attraction dies down, little will be left. They are walking a dead-end road.

I am still in contact with Doris. She and Gerhard even visited us once. I will not give them up. I shall try to lead them away from the dead-end road, but it will be a difficult task since I have neither their parents nor her doctors on my side.

The phrase *accident rate* from the mouth of a woman doctor to a young girl who is supposed to become a mother some day, disturbs me deeply. New life, an accident! What have we come to?

One of Doris's statements gives the answer: "I only believe in God as long as I need him." This means that she does not believe in God. She has no antenna for the fact that the Creator has meant her for marriage and that only in this context is the gift of sexuality full of meaning.

If she continues to live the way she does, she is going to pay a high price—more than a hundred dollars. It is expensive to live against the laws of creation.

Doris's boyfriend tried to force physical closeness and lost more that he gained. How differently Reinhard, the next correspondent, treats the girl he meets!

"A girl friend has to be kissed"
2

"At that time, I thought that a girl friend absolutely had to be kissed. . . . I imagined that I was a famous rock singer. . . . Tell me what I can do in order not to fall back into dreaming."
Reinhard H., age 16, high-school student

Dear Mr. Trobisch,

A year ago I bought and read your book *Love Is a Feeling to Be Learned.* I do not agree with everything you say in this book. In spite of that I hope to get your confidence, and I hope you can help me. Here's my story and my problem:

A few weeks ago I became sixteen. I'm a high-school student. In April and May of this year I had my first girl friend. She was two months older, but shorter than I am. Her name is Christine. She goes to the same school as I do. We saw each other often and finally I fell in love with her and she with me.

At that time I thought that a girl friend absolutely had to be kissed. Therefore I was very happy when, after about three weeks, I kissed Christine. In the following two weeks, I kissed her three, four or five times because I was then still very shy.

One day she told me that she wanted to break up with me. It was after we had gone steady for five weeks. I was very sad and started to daydream. In my dreams I imagined that I was a famous rock singer and being famous made me popular with girls. Then Christine would come back to me.

After that I went with Anne. She was two years younger than Christine, but somehow looked more feminine. This attracted me at that time. We kissed rather often, met in the woods and I stroked her hands and face.

After five weeks it was I who did not want to continue. I thought everything was going too quickly. When she kissed me I didn't feel anything anymore.

In October I took dancing lessons with my classmates. There I met a very nice girl. Every time I could choose my partner I danced with her. When we met on a Sunday we walked arm in arm. But then at the next dancing class she told me that she just wanted to dance with me, but not get involved in a deeper relationship.

Again I started to daydream.

In school I saw Christine, my first girl friend whom I still loved. I dreamt that we were together again.

On November 9th I met with her and asked her to go with me again. She refused saying that she already had a boyfriend, but at the moment he was in the hospital.

Four days later she came to me at school and asked whether I would go with her again. We started going arm in arm, but we did not kiss because in the meantime I had come to the conclusion that a girl friend is not just someone to be kissed. She is also someone with whom you can discuss your problems and enjoy being with. Just being with her is enough to make me happy.

When I saw her today she told me her boyfriend had called her and said that he would beat her up when he got out of the hospital. That's why she said she couldn't go out with me anymore. This story doesn't sound very feasible, but I believe it because I love Christine.

Please tell me what I can do in order not to fall back into dreaming. Write me too what I can tell Christine so that she won't hurt other boys as much as she has me.

Please answer as soon as possible. Please seal the envelope well because I can't tell my parents anything about it.
Many greetings,
Reinhard

Dear Reinhard,

The most important insight that you gained is that a girl is not simply an object to be kissed, but a person with whom you can talk over serious things. In the first period of your relationship with girls you considered Christine more or less a toy and Anne probably too.

You have also learned that too much kissing can make you numb. Therefore it is wise to be very sparing with kisses. A kiss is like money. It loses value if there's too much of it around. Furthermore, a girl usually appreciates feeling kissable more than actually being kissed.

When you met Christine the second time and began your friendship again but did not kiss her, you didn't see her anymore as a toy, but as a human being. This was a great step in the direction of maturity.

You are still on the road to this goal. But I have to tell you something very sobering. As beautiful as they may seem, those feelings of love which you feel now are not yet real love. You are basically projecting your own image onto the girl and the girl is doing the same. The magic will continue only as long as the other one corresponds to this dream image. Sooner or later the magic will disappear and then the inevitable disappointment will come.

Christine has evidently had this experience before you. Perhaps this is because at your age, girls are often ahead of boys in their development. This explains why Christine seems to prefer a boy one or two years older than herself.

There is no way to avoid pain. Lover's grief is necessary and you have to learn to live with it. You cannot save yourself from it, nor Christine, nor the other boys. This coming and going of acquaintances and friendships with all its pain and all its happiness simply has to be lived through.

To a certain extent, daydreams also belong to this pain and happiness. You don't need to fight against them. The more mature you become and the more you discover yourself as you really are, the less you will have to flee into daydreaming.

The first step in finding this maturity is to turn your thoughts away from yourself and to try to think and feel as another person would think and feel. When you are more interested in the concerns and worries of someone else than you are in your own troubles, a real feeling of love is awakening within you.

Do you know what impressed me the most in your letter? That "very nice girl" you met at your dancing class, who told you clearly that she just wanted to dance with you, but not get involved in a deeper relationship. She's healthy and has the right spirit. She knows exactly what goes with her age and what does not. She knows how to keep the limits and how to live in harmony with her development.

That hurt you too. But it must hurt along with the rest. Otherwise you will not grow.

With cordial greetings,

W.T.

Reflection

As I have already said, Reinhard is much more careful in his approach to girls than was Doris's boyfriend. He is also very sensitive to that which is authentic and realizes immediately when a gesture becomes meaningless. His insight that talking can make his relationship to a girl closer than too early and too much fondling and kissing will help him to build a meaningful and lasting relationship later on.

Doris did not mention her parents at all in her first letter. Reinhard mentioned only that he cannot talk to them. This is

normal to a certain degree. Young people at this age do not like
to discuss such experiences with their parents. Nevertheless,
as his letter shows, Reinhard needs someone outside of the
family with whom he can communicate.

I was saddened by his plea for a well-sealed envelope. Do
his parents really have so little respect for him that they would
read his personal mail? This would be a great mistake for
parents of a sixteen-year-old son.

When I read the manuscript of this book to my children who
were then between fourteen and twenty-one years of age, they
thought my answer to Reinhard was too authoritarian. That is
why they wanted to know if Reinhard had answered and what
he had said.

It was almost a year before the answer came: "I have read
your letter many times. But I didn't answer because I didn't
have any special reason for writing back. The truth is, I am now
very happy, but it didn't seem to me that this would be reason
enough to write you. As time went by, my problem became
less and less of a burden for me. Although I still like one particular girl, since February I haven't had any more longing for her.
I believe I've learned much about friendships. . . ."

The next correspondence, with Elke K., describes from a
girl's point of view this hesitating, cautious approach to the
other sex.

"How can I find a real boyfriend?"
3

*"I've never had a real boyfriend. I pretend
to others that I'm happy not to have one. . . .
Please tell me . . . how I can finally find a real boyfriend."*
Elke K., age 16, high-school student

Dear Mr. Trobisch,

At the moment I'm reading your book *Love Is a Feeling to Be
Learned.* It interests me and I'm learning a lot. Yet it doesn't
seem to help me much personally. Please let me explain my
problem.

In two months I'll be seventeen. I've never had a real boyfriend. I pretend to others that I'm happy not to have one.
Although basically this is true, I realize there are times when I
would very much like to have a boyfriend.

I fall in love quite often. Don't ask me how deeply. I cannot
sleep for nights on end. I'm thinking **constantly** of him, dreaming of him and of sharing the future with him. Of course, the
poor guy has no idea about it because I would never reveal my
feelings to him.

Then when I wake up to reality after a few days and the
dream ends, my feelings change completely. I almost start
hating him. I think the reason for this is that in my dreams this

boy does everything I want him to do, while in reality he doesn't even notice me. How could he when he barely knows me by sight?

After going through such an experience I feel somehow disappointed. This has already happened to me with many, many boys. Please tell me as soon as you can how to avoid repeating this mistake and how I can finally find a real boyfriend.
Many thanks in advance,
Elke

Dear Elke,

In a masterful way you have succeeded in putting into words the burden of your age group: this strange hanging in between dream and reality—this feeling of happiness and unhappiness at the same time. You have to learn to live with that which is difficult. It simply belongs to being seventeen. I would deprive your life of richness if I were to take away from you those precious sleepless nights in which your soul is growing.

Something new is awakening in you, something as yet unknown to you—namely, your longing for the other sex. This longing is a good longing and a healthy one. It makes you move toward a great goal, "sharing the future" as you call it. That goal includes wholeness and fulfillment.

Yet at the same time your soul—I could also say your personality—is not yet strong enough to fulfill this longing. It is not yet able to establish a real relationship with someone from the other sex. It is just this which is difficult, for your soul is still en route, on its way. It is taking its first hesitant steps. It is in the process of learning how to walk. There is no other way to learn except simply to endure this conflict.

If I were to offer you a cut-and-dried solution, I would hinder your personality from developing. It is necessary to let the deep pain hurt and to suffer through the discords of dreaming and reality. You grow just because of this suffering. Somehow growth is usually connected with pain.

It is good that you can dream. While you dream your soul is working, bringing together longing and experience. But it is also good that you keep your dreams to yourself. A bottle of perfume must be kept tightly closed, or the fragrance is lost.

Those who try to translate their dreams too quickly and too cheaply into words or actions, fail. They destroy the fine tissues woven by this unhappy happiness. Would the boys of your age be able to understand if you tried to tell them how you really feel? I'm afraid it would be beyond them and they might only be tempted to abuse your precious longing.

This is why you are wise to be silent about your dreams. Let them be dreams without trying to break through the wall which separates them from reality.

You want a real boyfriend. Yes, you are entitled to this wish. But just what would a real boyfriend be like? One who would stand up for you in every situation? One on whom you can absolutely rely? One who protects you? One who trusts you and in whom you can confide everything? One who sees you as unique, the only one, and who would remain faithful to you for life? Isn't this true?

You can see what I'm getting at. Such a friend cannot yet be. No boy, even if he were a year or two older than you, could give this to you now. It would be unjust to demand it from anyone.

This is why the longing—this good and precious longing —has to remain a longing at least for the time being. You have to learn to live with unfulfilled desires. This is the difficult art of your time of life. If you learn this skill now you will have gained something for your whole life.

Maybe what you are looking for could be given to you by a good girl friend with whom you could share your innermost feelings—even your feelings of hate and aggression. Your observation is correct that the feelings of hate and love are very close together. It is indifference—not hatred—which is the opposite of love. You are good to have noticed this.

You hate this boy because he causes you pain and disappointment. And this is precisely because you are not indifferent to him. But your pain is a pain of growth, Elke, and therefore something good and healing. Basically, any disillusionment is something positive because it destroys the illusion that the dream could be reality and that you could experience something which in truth you cannot.

Therefore, the experience of hating is as much a part of the maturing process in which you now find yourself as is the experience of disillusionment which I may have caused by giving you this answer.

Yours,

W.T.

Dear Mr. Trobisch,

I would like to thank you from the bottom of my heart for your letter. I was relieved because I had thought that my thinking and feeling were wrong, even abnormal. I believe this is because of the many magazines and films we see today. They make us live in the illusion that true love is something which is only beautiful and simple. In reality it looks very different.

I have talked a lot about these problems with my older brother. He is the one with whom I can share best at the moment. It was also he who advised me to write to you.

But now I've done something really stupid. I wrote an anonymous letter to a boy whom I have not been able to get out of my thoughts for more than a year now. "Anonymous" is not quite the right word, because in the letter I gave him a hint so that he could figure out who had written the letter. I told him a little bit about myself and then asked him to try to find my address and answer my letter. I also wrote him that I expected him to keep the whole thing a secret between the two of us.

Today I know that this was a big mistake. In the first place,

he didn't answer and second, he made fun of me when talking to his friends. I know this because one of those friends told my brother.
Cordial greetings,
Elke

Reflection
Elke failed because of her half-hearted effort. She wants to take two steps at the same time. In this way, she oversteps the necessary phase of friendship between people of the same sex.

All of us go through three phases in our development. The first phase is called the *autoerotic* phase. *Autos* is the Greek word for "self." *Eros* is the Greek word for "love." In this phase we are in love with ourselves, not yet able to relate to someone else.

The autoerotic phase is followed by the *homoerotic* phase. *Homos* means "same." It is an in-between phase. On the one hand, we are able to direct our feelings to a "stranger," someone who is not "myself," and yet we are not mature enough to direct them to a representative of the other sex.

The third phase is called the *heteroerotic* phase. *Heteros* is the Greek word for "other" or "different." In this phase the person is mature enough to face the otherliness of the opposite sex, to relate to someone who is so "strange," so "different."

Elke has not yet reached this level of maturity. She would have been able to establish a healthy relationship with a girl friend, but her personality is not yet strong enough for a relationship with the opposite sex. Even though she dares to write a letter to a boy, she hides herself in it. The boy, of course, does not understand what causes such behavior and finds it funny, even ridiculous.

In this respect, the next letter is entirely different. It describes a conscious, direct approach between the sexes. Again we hear from a young man.

"My next girl friend will become my wife"
4

"I told several friends that my next girl friend would become my wife. . . . She's a Christian too and had asked the Lord for clear guidance. . . . Now I stand in front of a void."
Axel R., age 17, high-school student

Honorable Sir,

I just turned seventeen. For half a year now I've tried to be a Christian, and I realize that many things have changed in my life through Jesus. But now I'm at a point where I don't know how to proceed.

On New Year's Eve I became conscious of the fact that I sensed something for a certain girl. Her name is Katrine. I didn't take this too seriously at first, but then the feeling of love grew and captivated me.

I prayed to the Lord that he would take it in his hands. I also told him that I wished Katrine would feel something for me. I tried to be together with her as often as possible, but every attempt out of my own strength to get closer to her failed.

Maybe it was a dumb thing to do, but I told several friends that my next girl friend would become my wife. Very conscious of this statement, I realized Katrine could be this girl.

One day my friend told me that Katrine had said that she also liked me. That very same night we had our first talk together.

For four months I had been praying for this moment and now it had come. I told her how I felt about her, and she said that it was on New Year's Eve that lightning had struck. She's a Christian too and had asked the Lord for clear guidance. Now, I thought, I have found the wife meant for me by God!

Since both of us had just turned seventeen, a period of two years loomed suddenly before us. We decided not to deepen our friendship during these two years although we agreed that we would marry someday. Since I still have two years left of high school before I can go to college and seminary, we decided not to go steady nor have any physical contact during these two years.

I was quite determined to follow this plan. We never saw each other except in our youth group. We didn't show our feelings to each other. I was completely convinced that Jesus had given Katrine to me as my future wife.

Then one day my heart stopped beating. I don't understand anything anymore.

I'd been away on a trip for two weeks. When I got back we took a walk together but Katrine didn't even look or smile at me. She said that it was already the second time that she had no feelings at all for me. She was close to tears because she felt guilty.

She asked me to let the whole thing rest because she wanted a husband she felt love for every day of her life, not one she loved for just three months and twenty-eight days. That's how many days have passed since our first talk.

Now I stand in front of a void. I just can't understand why this happened. Is it because we decided not to kiss for two years? Or does God have still a better wife for me? Can God guide in this way? Or must I learn to be "down"? Have I been too hard on myself and on her? Are we too young?

"You make wise plans and you do mighty things; you see everything that people do and you reward them according to their actions" (Jer. 32:19).

I'm convinced that **God** guides me, but I'm at my wits' end and I'm confused. I'm so unsure. I pray that you will be able to help me. I believe that you can.

Yours,
Axel

Dear Axel,

Thank you for your letter. First I will answer your questions. It's very possible that God has another wife for you. Maybe Katrine was the second best, while God still has the first best in store for you.

Yes, God can guide in such a way. Yes, you do have to learn to be "down." This is the best preparation for life. It pays to suffer lover's grief precisely for this reason. In this way you become a man.

No, you haven't been too hard on yourself. It was dumb to announce to everyone that your next girl friend would become your wife. Your relationship certainly didn't go to pieces because you laid down such strict rules. On the contrary, it probably would have broken down sooner if you had gone too far. Imagine how embarrassing that would be for you now—especially if you think that someday you will meet God's first choice for you.

Yes, you are very young. You can't yet make a decision about marriage and you shouldn't even try. Both of you will change a lot between the ages of seventeen and twenty. Your feelings also are going to change. After three or four years you might not even be able to understand what attracted you so much to each other.

I believe that you should be very grateful to Katrine because she told you honestly how she feels and didn't play around with your feelings by pretending something just to make you happy. There are some girls who like to play with boys' feelings, just because they are a little ahead of the boys in their emotional development.

In a way, Katrine's honesty is a sign of love. The German poet Goethe says: "To renounce at the right moment is a sign of friendship. Love often does damage because it considers the desires of the beloved more than his happiness."

Love for you now means to fulfill Katrine's wish and let things be. Both of you need this rest after the storm in order to find yourselves. For one who is preparing for the ministry, it is particularly unwise to be bound too early by the chains of love. Because of the great demands placed upon her, a pastor's wife must be chosen with special care. Give yourself time for this choice.

Don't lose patience with yourself or with God. I am glad that you can bring all the decisions of your daily life to your Lord and that you count on him and his guidance in a very concrete way. God proves himself often as the one who makes "wise plans" when he cancels our human plans.

As far as I can see, God has already helped you. When he brings us to our wits' end and we feel as if we are standing in front of a complete void, then his way with us can begin.

Isn't it a beautiful and adventurous situation to stand in front of a void with unlimited possibilities ahead of you? It is just the void which contains the promise of the future.

Only the one who is broken can find the doors leading into the joy of Jesus Christ.

With kindest greetings,
W.T.

Reflection

When I read this correspondence to my sons, they found Axel's letter somehow exaggerated and unnatural. They thought Axel thinks too much and feels too little. They were also amused by his exact count of the days of his friendship with Katrine. This occurred also in Reinhard's letter when he reported in which week and how often he had kissed. Maybe this emphasis on data is an attempt on the part of the boys to render their feelings banal or trite.

Be that as it may, the important thing is that Axel relates his love experience to God. He refuses to be a boat without a rudder being steered by every wind that blows. Finding God's will in affairs of the heart is especially difficult. The experience of being overcome by such intense and awesome feeling is often taken to be God's voice or even God's action. This is why we often need someone from outside who can see it more objectively.

Axel's answer came ten months later: "At last I will answer your letter. I'm afraid you'll be disappointed. Soon after I got your letter the situation cleared up. I was ready to give up everything and then Katrine came to me out of her own accord.

"I was prepared for anything. I liked her again immediately when she came and I sensed that she cared for me too.

"We've been going steady now for over a year and are happy. There would have been many occasions to break up again, but our third partner is Jesus. We've put our relationship into his hands and that's our greatest help. Looking back, I can only say we are very thankful to God."

Two things in his letter I think are remarkable. The first is the fact that here a girl takes a step toward a boy out of her own accord. A girl does not always need to be passive and hide her feelings. Here the word of Jesus applies: "The truth shall make you free" (Jn. 8:32).

To act out of truth, though, means that the girl puts herself "in the light" and that she does not play hide-and-seek as Elke did. Acting out of truth takes ego-strength because she also risks being turned down. She would have to be strong enough to stand up under such an experience.

Second, it is remarkable that the two of them have excluded the physical realm for the time being. This they told me in a personal talk when I visited them. They consider this time a trial period, and they do not want to miss out on any growth experiences by starting a sexual relationship. They would rather draw the physical limits too narrow than too wide.

The wisdom of this decision is illustrated in the next correspondence. Again we meet two Christians.

"Klaus and I
stayed overnight
in the same room"
5

*"Klaus and I slept in one of those rooms.
During those two nights nothing
happened at all."*
Rita G., age 16, high-school student

Dear Mr. Trobisch,

My name is Rita G. I'm sixteen and a high school student. I just read your book *My Beautiful Feeling* and decided to write to you about my problem. I'm a Christian and have been active in youth work this past year in our town.

When I was fourteen, I had my first boyfriend. We went steady for a year. I put God aside during that time. When my boyfriend and I broke up, I had a very hard inner struggle to get really free from him. I didn't realize how deeply I had been emotionally involved. I was terribly disappointed and felt very bad.

Nine months ago I got acquainted with Klaus. He's nineteen and also a true believer. My mother knew about our friendship and she liked Klaus a lot. In April some fellows from our youth group, Klaus and I went skiing. We stayed overnight in a hut where there were only rooms with two beds each. Klaus and I slept in one of those rooms. During those two nights nothing happened at all. We lay beside each other encircling each other with our arms (which perhaps we shouldn't have done). I told this to my mother when she asked about it. She was very disappointed with us as were Klaus's parents.

Klaus had often come to pick me up for a date, but then it became less and less frequent. I tried to make it clear to him that my mother forgave him long ago, but he would not or could not believe it.

Two months later both of us were invited to a birthday party to be held at a hut in the mountains. We were both looking forward to it very much. But the day we were supposed to leave, Klaus came to me very depressed and said his parents wouldn't allow him to go. I was very mad at his parents after he left. Without thinking it over, I went to one of Klaus's cousins and asked him to take me along. He did. Klaus was terribly disappointed in me which I can very well understand.

After we got back home from the party I realized that Klaus didn't show up anymore at our house. When I asked him why, he told me that he couldn't forget what had happened and that the other boys made fun of him. He had decided to break up even though he said he still loved me.

Is this my fault? Why can't Klaus forgive and forget? I just can't shake myself free from him. I love him just as much as ever if not more. We haven't yet talked about everything. I don't know how he feels. Shall I try to talk to him again or should I do nothing? I have the feeling that he loves me, but he doesn't want to face it. If we meet in a group, he's just friendly and nice to me. Could you please help me?

Many thanks that you listened to me and that I could write to you,
Rita

Dear Rita,

Thanks a lot for your letter. I especially appreciated the fact that you also told me when you had failed.

You say that you are a Christian and active in youth work. Also you say that Klaus is a true believer. If you take the word *believe* seriously in its deepest meaning, then it means to recognize something as authentic and valid. It does not mean, as so many think, to take something for the truth which cannot be proven. Believing is an action which has binding consequences. One of these consequences is a certain lifestyle from which others can conclude that the action of believing has taken place in the life of this person and is taking place daily.

I'm of the opinion that staying overnight in the same room or the same tent does not belong to this lifestyle. It is a marital situation which belongs to the context of what the Bible calls "to become one flesh." According to biblical thinking this situation is exclusively related to marriage.

By putting yourself in compromising situations, you are doing something which does not correspond to being a Christian—even if "nothing" happens. By *nothing* I take it you mean the sexual union or some sexual play. Even if this does not happen, something else does happen. Strong desires are aroused which you must suppress very strongly. If you suppress these over and over again it is hard to correct later on.

I respect Klaus highly. Evidently he's not just disappointed in you, but also in himself because he's made a compromise with his standards. Looking at it from this point of view something must have happened for which he can hardly forgive himself. That's why he drew the line. I think highly of such an attitude. Also, he obeyed his parents even though it meant giving up his own wishes. He did this despite the fact that he is nineteen. Compare this to the way you disappointed your mother even though you are only sixteen.

He probably also realized that the friendship with you goes beyond the strength of both of you and brings you into situations which you cannot handle. I think he did the right thing when he broke up with you—maybe just because he likes you and wants the best for you.

Right now you can't do anything else but accept it. It's good for you to learn to live at a distance and still to be friendly toward each other. This is an art and Klaus is giving you a good example.

You have to pay a price for acting without thinking. If you want to develop a lifestyle from which others can conclude that you are a Christian, it is not possible to act without thinking. As Christians we are not only responsible for our actions but also for our reputation. Therefore it's important that we do not give impressions which can lead others to wrong conclusions.

In this age of permissiveness, anyone who knows that you spent two nights together in the same room would take it for granted that you had sex. That's why such behavior is no testimony for your Lord.

I'm glad that you admit your mistake and that you can even understand Klaus's disappointment about you. The only real mistakes in life, however, are the ones from which we do not learn.
Cordial greetings,
W.T.

Dear Mr. Trobisch,

It's quite a while [six months later] since I wrote you. The friendship with Klaus is finished. I apologized to him, he's forgiven me, but he says he can't forget. We see each other every Friday in our youth group, but this doesn't mean a thing. There are times when I become very depressed if I see him and I even think of suicide. At present I'm getting medical treatment for an ulcer caused by the nervous strain of this relationship.

Klaus has a very strict father who does not allow his children much freedom for the simple reason: "We were not allowed to do it either."
Rita

Reflection

A brief word about the last paragraph of Rita's letter is in order. It is one of the rare cases in which a father who acts, interferes, directs and stands up for his opinion is mentioned.

The only trouble is, he doesn't talk. The reason which he gives to his children is insufficient. He forces his children to obey without insight and this is not enough.

Why must the strong father always behave as a patriarch? What we need today are fatherly fathers—neither patriarchal nor marginal. Is this really so difficult?

Hans, writer of the next letter, is able to talk to his father but they do not seem to be able to get to the heart of matters. It was from Hans that I received this letter of protest.

"Even one girl is too many"
6

*"Had I known how many complications
your book would cause, . . . I never
would have read it. . . . The way you talk about
caressing makes me sick. . . ." "I wouldn't like to
marry a girl who has already slept with five
or six boys."*
Hans K., age 14, high-school student

Dear Sir:
Through an acquaintance I got your book *Love Is a Feeling to Be Learned*. Since the title interested me, I read it and then passed it on to several other friends my age, namely fourteen years old.

Had I known how many complications your book would cause and how base I would feel after reading it, I never would have read it.

I don't want to criticize your basic ideas or even put them down, but the hardness you used in expressing yourself I find simply irresponsible. According to your book, a girl who is not chaste is more or less a prostitute. If you sleep together before marriage, it's a great sin, and the marriage can't be saved anymore. The way you talk about caressing makes me sick.

After I'd read your book, I was very unsure. Of course, there's no question that friendships can suffer under things like that. Over and over again I wish that I'd never read the book. The others who read it say the same.

Everything goes wrong in your book. None of the contraceptives are safe. If a boy sleeps with a girl, he usually leaves her in the lurch. Why did you present everything in this book in such a pessimistic way?

I would be very thankful for a prompt answer.

With friendly greetings,
Your Hans

Dear Hans:

Many, many thanks for your letter. I think it is good that you blew your top and that you told me frankly what you think about my book.

Did you ask yourself why the book made you angry? I'll tell you why: because it made you have a bad conscience. Or maybe this bad conscience, this feeling of being on the wrong track was already there and my book only confirmed it.

If you are angry because the book made you feel base or vile, maybe it is because you had to face the truth. Maybe you did indeed act in a base or vile manner.

It hurts to admit this yourself, I know. But sometimes it can be the greater love to hurt someone even though he gets angry.

This leads to your question as to why I presented the negative consequences so realistically—not pessimistically, as you say. I did it because I have literally hundreds of letters here in my office which testify to the way people's lives have been fouled up because they transgressed God's commandments. Unfortunately, it's true that the unhappiness of many marriages begins with an unhealthy premarital conduct. If your present friendship with your girl friend suffers now under your own insecurity, that is still better than if your marriage suffers later. I have expressed myself as clearly and as hard as possible out of a sense of responsibility precisely to warn of trouble and to prevent disaster.

It could be, of course, that your experiences are different.

Then please share them with me. I wish, though, that your girl friend would also tell me what she thinks about my book. As a matter of fact, I have a lot of grateful letters from girls. Some have even written: "If I had read your book one day earlier, my life would not have been fouled up."

Sad to say, but it does happen quite often that a boy leaves a girl in the lurch after he has conquered her sexually. I am glad that you, evidently, do not belong to this group and I greet you cordially.

Yours,

W.T.

Dear Sir,

First of all I want to thank you for your nice letter and at the same time correct an error. I must tell you the truth: I didn't write that first letter to you at all. It was my girl friend who wrote it. She wrote it using my name and my address because she was afraid her parents would read your answer and scold her.

This means that the first letter actually contained the thoughts of my girl friend, but you couldn't know this.

I have to admit you are right. Many boys do leave a girl in the lurch after she has given herself to them completely. But I also know a number of boys where this was not the case.

I certainly am not in favor of a girl going to bed with just any boy. I wouldn't like to marry a girl who has already slept with five or six boys.

On the other hand, I think—and I talked about it with my parents who agreed with me—that it's perfectly all right to be friends with two or three girls before marriage.

I believe though that it is only in marriage that you really get to know a girl or a woman. If you marry the first girl you meet, you are still inexperienced and then in the long run you may be disappointed because it doesn't turn out like you think it will. And then the marriage can break up. This is bad especially if there are children. Besides that you are transgressing God's commandment not to commit adultery.

Maybe my opinion is completely wrong, because it also says in the Bible that God wants to keep sexual relations for marriage. Still, I think it's better to have had two or three girls before marriage than to commit adultery once you are married.
Cordial greetings,
Hans

Dear Hans,

What I like about your letter is that you have an unusual gift at your age of being able to look ahead and to judge things from the perspective of the goal to be reached.

You already have marriage or the possible failure of marriage in view in deciding how you will act now.

Of course, everything depends on what you mean by the words "to be friends." Possibly your parents do not agree with you here. If you mean by being friends, to get closely acquainted, I would say that two or three girls are not enough. One has to get acquainted with many girls before one can really choose.

But if by being friends you mean sleeping together, then I would say that even one girl is too many. I am of this opinion precisely because of the goal. It has been proven that in those marriages where both partners have not known anyone else sexually before marriage, unfaithfulness is rarest.

If one or two would be all right, why not five or six? Your arguments become inconsistent here.

It is a fact that sexual experiences before marriage turn out to be more of a burden than a help later on. They can become a stumbling block to knowing girl friends in a deeper way and even disturb the sexual union in marriage. The fact that change has become a habit and comparison is possible has a negative effect on marriage.

Do you really think your girl friend, who wrote the first letter to me, would become a good wife if she keeps on the way she is going? By the way, her parents don't seem to be in agreement with her. Otherwise she wouldn't have been worried that they might read my answer.

It is dangerous to put your own norms above God's norms. Remember it was not human meanness which crucified the Son of God but human arrogance trying to be wiser than God.
I greet you very cordially,
W.T.

Reflection
The correspondence with Hans brings out a very important problem: the privacy of our children's mail. Hans does not say how old his girl friend is, but I would judge she is sixteen at the most.

To me there is no question that parents should respect the privacy of their children's mail at this age. It is understandable that parents want to protect their children from negative influences, but this is not the way to do it. They tempt their children to become dishonest and force them to use sneaky means to protect their privacy, as the letter of Hans's girl friend illustrates. Besides that they give their children the feeling that they do not trust them and underestimate their ability to judge. This is one of the reasons why these children may not turn to their parents when they need help. Once confidence is broken down, it is hard for parents to exercise influence on their children.

The greatest protection parents can give to their children is the inner certainty: "My parents trust me to make the right decision." In contrast to his girl friend's parents, Hans's parents seem to respect the privacy of his letters. Maybe this is why they are able to talk things over with him even though their talks seem to be rather superficial.

Another conclusion we can draw from Hans's letter is that it is by no means too early to talk with a fourteen-year-old about marriage. Certainly when he tries to form his opinions, the pressure of his peer group is at work. Here parents who themselves have a firm standpoint could create a good counterweight by daring to discuss very concrete questions, such as that of pregnancy and contraceptives. Hans does not even seem to think of these possible problems.

Hans is especially mistaken when he thinks that preparing for marriage means getting ready for the sexual act. Of one hundred hours of married life, one might be spent in sexual relations. It is the other ninety-nine hours which need preparation.

The next correspondent is even younger than Hans, only thirteen. Yet she has a boyfriend who is almost nineteen. She does not appear to even think of having sex with him. Rather, her sexual problems are centered in herself. That which Borghild is seeking and cannot find is a place of security, the experience of being sheltered.

"Is masturbation a sin?"
7

*"Does Jesus have anything against a
friendship at the age of thirteen? . . . Is masturbation a sin? I can't help it—especially
when I need love. . . . I eat and eat. Sometimes
I really stuff myself."*
Borghild H., age 13   boyfriend, age 18

Dear Mr. Trobisch,

I write to you because I'm looking for an answer.

I'm thirteen. You'll be surprised that I write to you. It's because of how old I am that I'm doing it. Too much so?

I have a boyfriend. He will be nineteen in two months. We
understand each other in a really unique way. Really! We are
both Christians. He's working as a medical aid. My parents, yes,
my whole family including grandpa and our dog, accept him.
He belongs to us. He visits us very often.

Now I believe one thing is important: We've known each
other for six months. I want to ask you, does Jesus have anything against a friendship at the age of thirteen? Does he have
anything against holding hands? No more?

Oh boy, now I'll just say what's on my heart. I hope you have
time to read it.

They all think that I'm still too young and seem to agree with
the saying: One kiss is already the first step into bed. Oh boy,
that really makes me depressed!

Something else: Is masturbation a sin? I can't help it—especially when I need love. Then I tell myself quickly, "Jesus loves you more than all else." But when I say I'm a Christian it's hard to believe, isn't it? Or is it?

I hope this letter reaches you. I do hope so. I want an answer so very much! Please! Many thanks!

Yours,
Borghild

P.S. I'm going to leave this letter just as it is. If I write it over again I would leave something out.

Dear Borghild,

Thank you for your letter written from your heart. Of course you can be friends with a young man and hold hands, but inwardly you will not gain very much. Because of your age difference, it will be difficult to meet at the same level. At your age it would be more important to have a good girl friend.

I'm afraid that the tensions which go along with having a boyfriend will cost you too much strength at your age. A kiss will not necessarily lead into bed. Yet there is a bit of truth in that saying. Actually my wife and I have answered these questions in our book *My Beautiful Feeling*. It's a correspondence with a seventeen-year-old girl, who, by the way, also struggled with the problem of masturbation. In this book we tried to answer the difficult question of whether or not it is a sin. Maybe you could get hold of it and then write to us and tell us whether you could identify with any of it.

Yes, you made a very fine observation when you said that you are looking for love, or rather the feeling of being loved, when you masturbate. But precisely in this way you will not find it.

Write again!
Your W.T.

Dear Mr. Trobisch,

I'm really very grateful that you answered me. I read the book and really I have the same problems as Ilona.

Even with eating I have the same difficulties. I eat and eat. Sometimes I really stuff myself.

Even though I do this, I'm really very slim. Everyone says this about me. My mother thinks I almost worship my body. It goes like this: There are times when I'm not disciplined at all with eating. At other times I am, but then my stomach grumbles all day long. When I want to become slim, I stand in front of my mirror naked every night.

Every time I hear this same little voice as when I masturbate. It says: "But Borghild, it doesn't make any difference to God whether you are slim or not. God loves you anyway. You may eat as much as you want." And then I do precisely that which I do not want to do. Can you help me? Please do.

I cannot give up masturbation. Before it happens I have almost a joy of expectation: "Oh, finally a chance to flee out of the humdrum of daily life—to really show love to myself!"

Oh prunes! I really have a hard time expressing myself. I hope you have time. Honestly, I really don't want to bother you.

Mom says I shouldn't even think about "such things." (Please, I don't want to give my mother a bad grade!)

And now the problem with the jeans. We had a scene again today about it. She said, "At least when you go to church, don't wear those jeans."

I admit they are rather worn out. It's only this one pair of jeans that I wear every day. Okay! To please my mother I wore another pair but my good mood was destroyed. In the afternoon I was then permitted to wear the old ones again and I really felt better. That's the way it is!

Girls' clothes make me nauseated, even though I find femininity beautiful in others, yes, even attractive. I've felt really funny during the last weeks. Whenever I think now of marriage, intercourse, even friendship, it's too much. It even makes me want to vomit. I get really mad whenever I see lovers together. (In former times I wanted to get married. It was my only goal.) Do you know I really would like to break up with Manfred?

When I wrote my last letter to you it was still different. I wanted to be caressed, fondled. Twice we've said to each other, "I like you." When we said it the second time we touched briefly with our hands, but now I don't even want that anymore.

You know, I would like to be free and enjoy life. That's why marriage is suddenly so unattractive to me. Just imagine one's whole life with one and the same man.

Tell me, should I really break up with Manfred? I can barely stand to see him. I'm at my wits' end.

Mommy says she feels it wouldn't be fair to push him away just like that. I shouldn't have started with him in the first place.

At the beginning of our relationship, after one week, I already tried to break up with him because I wasn't sure our relationship was right before God. But then he was so sad that he convinced me. So we stuck together.

People raise their eyebrows when they see us together and this makes me uneasy. (On the other hand, there are nice sides to it too.)

Okay, if you have time, would you answer? Indeed, that would really be . . . , THANKS!
Yours,
Borghild

P.S. I've written everything straight from the heart. That's why I'm thankful beyond words.

Dear Borghild,

I'm also thankful that you write everything straight from your heart. Your expression *straight from the heart* has a very deep meaning. Inner conflicts and tensions can affect the heart and make you physically sick, especially if they are not expressed and the anger is swallowed up instead of being spit out. This can literally affect the heart. That's why it makes me very happy that you are able to get mad when you see lovers and that you also express your negative feelings about Manfred. To me this means that you are real. You have stopped playing a role which you think everyone expects from you, that is, that you must have a boyfriend because others in your age group might have one. You are honest about these negative feelings and you are yourself. Don't be ashamed of your feelings. Stand up for them and act accordingly.

Yes, you should really be free and enjoy life. That's just the reason why you should feel free to break up with Manfred.

Don't act against your conviction and make compromises. Stand up for what you think. Don't be swayed by the sadness of Manfred. That's his problem, not yours. He must learn to suffer grief without breaking down, and this is the only way to learn. In the final analysis you actually help him by being honest. "Love rejoices in the truth" (1 Cor. 13:6). This is what it says in the great chapter about love in the New Testament. Love is never an opponent of truth. It's an ally. Therefore sometimes love has to cause pain. Truth is always right before God. A compromise made out of pity is never right.

Truth, however, means that you live in accordance with your age. If you say, "I can't stand it anymore" and "I'm at my wits' end," then you are expressing exactly what a healthy girl of your age feels. No one can demand that you, at the age of thirteen, handle all the tensions which normally go hand in hand with a friendship. No one can expect either that at your age you be enthusiastic about marriage or that you even understand fully what it is or should be.

To have a deep friendship with a girl, though, would be just the thing for you now. It could be part of your freedom and enjoyment of life. It could set you free from turning around on your own axis and looking constantly at yourself in the mirror.

Nothing else could help you more to stop masturbating, which is only an expression of this turning around yourself.

We're happy that you have read our book about the subject and that you can identify with Ilona.

Basically, masturbation, eating too much or too little and even the bit about wearing old jeans are all symptoms of the same problem. You have not accepted yourself completely yet. Nor have you accepted yourself fully as a girl. In my book *Love Yourself,* you can see how these two are related.

But while you struggle with these symptoms, very softly another Borghild is awakening within you, coming out of her shell. It is the Borghild who finds "femininity beautiful" and who some years from now will become a young woman, an attractive young lady gracefully gliding across the floor in a long dress.

Up until this point you still have a long way to go and you must have patience with yourself. All these things—that you feel funny, that feelings, sometimes nausea, sometimes deep longing, get hold of you and conflict with each other—belong to your time of life. It will all clear up later on, but you have to take a step at a time and not miss any of the stages. Because God has patience with you, you can also have it with yourself.

But it's just this dimension I feel your letter lacks. Here's where you are different than Ilona. She didn't run away from God but faced up to his challenge. This is the step you have not yet taken. You listen too much to other voices—your mother, your friend, people. It doesn't matter whether people raise their eyebrows about your conduct or not, but whether God does.

If you face up to God's challenge and listen to him and him alone, he will not raise his eyebrows, but let his face shine on you and open the door to freedom and enjoyment, enabling you to stand above the humdrum of everyday life.

I would so much like to give evidence of his love to you. It is my heartfelt wish that some day you will enter this door. . . .
Kindest greetings,
W.T.

Reflection

Borghild is so real! So straightforward! She is still very much in the autoerotic phase. Masturbation, admiring her body in front of the mirror, wearing only jeans—all these belong in this context. She does not yet know who she is.

Of course, my correspondence with her cannot be completely understood without reading *My Beautiful Feeling* which she read between her first and second letters. You can see how she has grown through it. "Bibliotherapy," being healed through reading, has been effective in her life.

At the same time, Borghild is just in the beginning of the homoerotic phase. Her danger is that she might jump this stage and approach the other sex too soon due to peer pressure. Her mother seems to intensify this pressure without giving her enough help. The advice she gives Borghild, not to occupy her mind with such things, is of course insufficient.

Borghild is lucky that she has a friend like Manfred who evidently does not take advantage of her longing for tenderness, for shelter and for other proofs of love.

But where is the father who could and should give all of this to his thirteen-year-old daughter? Why isn't he even mentioned?

My wife says that she can understand Borghild's mother, who seems to think: better Manfred as my daughter's friend than someone else. Borghild is well taken care of by him. She would probably not find a young man like him so easily again.

Something in Borghild struggles against this relationship and she would like to break it off. Her mother does not seem to have an antenna for Borghild's healthy resistance. Why does she not even think of suggesting that Borghild find a good girl friend? Or why does she not try herself to be a friend to her daughter?

And how does the whole thing look from Manfred's point of view? Why does he go with such a young girl? One of my sons suggested that for many boys a girl is a sort of status symbol, like having a motorbike or a car. At Manfred's age, he would simply have to have one and if he is not strong enough inwardly to relate to a girl his own age, then at least he can relate to a younger one.

The problems of Joela B., the next correspondent, are very similar. She has neither a father nor a friend. On the other hand, she has a very understanding mother who does not intrude on her privacy and who can wait patiently until she finds herself.

Joela, though, began earlier than Borghild to masturbate, possibly about the time she lost her father through divorce.

"I would like to shoot my cycle off to the moon"

8

*"I've read many times already that masturbation
is not harmful, but this doesn't help me. . . .
It would be the eighth wonder of the world
if I would wear a skirt. . . . If I had my way, I would
like to shoot my whole cycle and everything
that goes with it off to the moon."*
Joela B., age 14, no father and no friend

Dear Mr. and Mrs. Trobisch,

My name is Joela and I'm fourteen. Some time ago I read your book *I Loved a Girl.* It impressed me a lot that the young African Francois discussed his problem with you so frankly. I've wanted to talk over my problems with someone now for a long time.

About four or five years ago I started to masturbate. It was only recently that I learned what I was really doing. Since then I have felt terribly ashamed. Am I normal? Is this a sign of being sick? I would like to get rid of it.

I believe in God and I've brought my problem to him in prayer. But nothing has changed. Did I do something wrong?

I've read many times already that masturbation is not harmful, but this doesn't help me. I can't talk about it with my mother, even though I think she knows about it.

I don't have a father, because my parents got divorced when I was still very young. Up until I was ten I had a wonderful relationship with my mother, but lately I feel like I'm always under attack and then I get really vicious. I don't want to be this way at all. I feel best when the atmosphere at home is peaceful and harmonious. Can you help me? May I write to you? If I'm really honest, I don't have much hope that I will receive an answer.

Thank you anyway that I could unburden myself on paper.
Cordial greetings,
Your Joela

Dear Joela,

It is good that you unburdened yourself on paper. This was certainly a step in the right direction. We would like to send you our book *My Beautiful Feeling,* which will answer many of your questions. We'd also like to know whether your mother respects the privacy of your mail. We hope she does for we are sure she would like to help you too, just as we would, and this is only possible if we can write very frankly.

I had just written this sentence when I discovered that you had put your phone number on your envelope, so I called you. Now we have even talked together! I'm glad that your mother does not open your letters and that she seems to understand that it is embarrassing to talk to one's own mother about this special problem.

Even though we are sending our book to you, we would like to answer your main question very briefly. You do not need to feel ashamed. You are very normal. You are not sick. It is true, masturbation (M.) is not harmful, but this does not mean that it is wholesome. Somehow you feel this yourself. In any case, masturbation is not a mature and meaningful way to deal with your sexuality.

Although it is certainly not a disease, it is a symptom of a deeper problem. Very often this problem is loneliness. It could very well be that there is a connection with the fact that you do not have a father. For a girl, it also often has to do with the relationship to her mother. Your letter seems to confirm this. Probably you would be much less tempted to do it if everything were peaceful and harmonious at home.

But this is enough for today. Write again after you have read the book.

Yours,

Walter and Ingrid Trobisch

Dear Mr. and Mrs. Trobisch,

Please don't be offended that I didn't write for such a long time. I had such a funny feeling somehow after I got your letter. You were not anymore an anonymous answerer of letters, but—excuse the comparison—you were so near, so close. Somehow I was a little bit afraid. I cannot really describe my feeling.

Many thanks for your letter and the phone call. It really was a happy surprise for me.

On the phone you asked me to write down the practical conclusions I drew from reading the book. One thing is that I thought of giving myself a sort of reward when I do not give in to the desire of M. (Sorry to say this doesn't happen very often.) I have started to draw and paint. This is a lot of fun.

By the way I have the same problem as Ilona. Nothing captivates or fascinates me completely. You write that in this way a vacuum is created. This is exactly the way I feel. Even though I like drawing, in the long run it doesn't give me complete fulfillment. I also have a little bit of a bad conscience when I draw because I always think, "You really should be studying now."

There's one thing which I really haven't understood yet. What does wearing jeans have to do with the fact of whether or not I accept myself as a girl? How can I learn to accept myself?

As a matter of fact, I always run around in jeans. My girl friend said recently, it would be the eighth wonder of the world if

I showed up wearing a skirt. I guess she's right.

You also told Ilona that she should live consciously with her cycle. I can't do that. If I had *my* way, I would like to shoot my whole cycle and everything that goes with it off to the moon. When I have my period, I can't do anything—not go swimming or any other sports. Besides that I always get terrible stomach pains. Why is it so important to live consciously with it?

Recently, M. happened quite often in comparison to summer vacation when it rarely happened. During the past week it didn't happen at all, until last night. Then I had no will to resist and the guilt feeling was there again.

Many thanks that I can write to you,
Your Joela

Dear Joela,

Thank you again for your frank letter. We see that you read our book quite thoroughly and you drew good conclusions. The idea of rewarding yourself is a good one. Maybe you should also reward yourself when you have done your homework by sketching and painting so that you don't need to have a bad conscience. How about doing it this way: for every hour of study you allow yourself fifteen minutes of painting. You also mentioned sports and swimming in passing. Maybe there are other things you really like to do. Don't you play an instrument?

One thing is for sure: nothing is more important for you right now than to take time to do the things you really enjoy. That will make studying easier too. You have seen for yourself that during summer vacation when you had lots of fun and no pressure, masturbation stopped completely.

One root cause of masturbation in your case is the lack of enthusiasm and joy. Another cause can be your lack of self-acceptance.

To accept yourself means to say yes to yourself—to the uniqueness with which God has created you. This means saying yes to your own characteristics, the age you are, how you look, your figure, your abilities and even lack of abilities in certain things. It certainly means saying yes to your sexuality.

Honestly, wouldn't you sometimes secretly prefer to be a boy? We can't help but read this between the lines of your letter. It could be that tomboyish girls or even girlish boys attract you at the moment.

This is normal at your age. It has a simple biological reason. At present you may have just about the same amount of male hormones as you have female hormones in your developing body. This will change later on and the female hormones will outnumber the others. Then you must decide whether you want to express your femininity or repress it. Repressing it will probably only intensify masturbation, but expressing it could bring you so much fulfillment that masturbation becomes unattractive.

One way to express it is by the way you dress. You feel like wearing only jeans at the moment, and this may correspond to your state of development. Besides that, from many points of view they really are more practical.

Someday you will discover that your body is created in such a way that a beautiful dress or a skirt and blouse is simply more becoming to you. And then you will be proud and glad to be a girl.

We think that those who try to eliminate the differences between the sexes do this out of fear. They are afraid of the otherliness of the opposite sex. Their egos are not strong enough to stand up under the tension created by the differences. If this tension is removed the relationship between the sexes becomes dull and insipid. This is one of the reasons why so many marriages become monotonous and unattractive. Often women who deny their femininity choose male partners who deny their masculinity.

But to accept your femininity means to accept your cycle. You simply can't shoot it off to the moon, because it belongs to you in the same way that your sexuality belongs to you. Maybe your stomach pains occur precisely because you wish you could get rid of your cycle, and you know that you're unable to do it.

From your letter we have the impression that when you use the word *cycle* you are thinking only of menstruation. There is much more involved to it than that. It is the whole miraculous process which happens in your body from one menstruation to the next. Different female hormones take the upper hand at different times. This can influence how you feel—the good, hopeful moods when you say you could conquer the whole world.

Ingrid has described this in detail in her book *The Joy of Being a Woman.* Maybe you are still a little young to read the whole book, but in the first and third chapters you will find a lot of things which can help you to live consciously and agreeably with and not against your cycle.

One day you will discover that as a woman you are rich—much richer than a man. Just remember that your cycle also has something to do with your ability to become a mother, the gift of bearing a child.

Write again!

Walter and Ingrid Trobisch

Reflection

It just happened that I had a speaking engagement in the vicinity of Joela's hometown, so I paid a visit to her and her mother about a year after this correspondence took place. I found myself in a comfortable home with a warm atmosphere. Everything was neat and arranged with good taste. Joela had a beautiful room of her own where she felt at home.

Her mother left me alone with Joela without asking any questions about the reason for my visit or the subject of our conversation. She has evidently stood up valiantly under the aggressive moods of her daughter without panicking.

When I talked with Joela, it became clear that she had overcome completely the immature habit of masturbation. She said that two things had helped her especially. One was our correspondence. "Simply the fact that someone knew about it without getting shocked was a big help," she said. "I wasn't alone with it any more."

The other thing that helped her was finding a good girl friend, a little bit older than she, with whom she could talk over everything that was on her heart.

This illustrates that, at this age, masturbation is mostly a sign of loneliness. In the following correspondence with Matthias we can see the same thing.

"I'm a loner"
9

"Up till now I've had to struggle with my problems . . . all by myself. . . . I'm a loner and suffer because I'm so shy around people. . . . It's only in this letter that I could express my thoughts frankly for the first time. . . . About two years ago I started to masturbate."
Matthias Z., age 16, fatherless

Dear Sir,

I have read your book *Love Is a Feeling to Be Learned*. I was very touched by it. This is why I turn to you with my desperate problem.

I'm sixteen and have a mother and a sister, twenty-seven years old. My father died four days after I was born. Neither my mother nor my sister have talked to me about the facts of life and up till now I've had to struggle with my problems in this realm all by myself. There's no one I can talk to about my problems. I'm a loner and suffer because I'm so shy around people. I don't believe I could talk with anyone openly.

It's only in this letter that I could express my thoughts frankly for the first time, because I believe, that is, I hope, you understand my problem.

About two years ago I started to masturbate. I simply wanted to try it once. I don't really know why. I always feel terribly ashamed afterward but still I do it again and again. My will is simply not strong enough to stop. It was so bad that I even tried to run away. For this reason I was put in a boarding school half a year ago. Unfortunately, that didn't help either.

I really don't know what to do, because I want to become a normal human being. Actually I'm ashamed to write this letter, but I can see a possibility of overcoming this problem by your advice. Please help me!
Yours,
Matthias

Dear Matthias,

Thank you very much for **your** frank letter. You certainly do not need to be ashamed. As a preliminary I'm sending you a book which I wrote with my wife. Even though it deals with a girl, the advice given in it about masturbation is also valid for boys. Please read it first and then write again.
Cordial greetings,
W.T.

Dear Sir,

Many, many thanks for your words and for the book *My Beautiful Feeling.*

I've read it twice in the meantime and could identify with most of the things you say in it. I am sorry that I didn't write sooner, but I thought because of the insights gained through this book I could overcome this problem. I'm sad to say this is not the case. Yesterday I did it again for the first time. I don't know why, but it simply happened.

Now I shall try to put into practice your advice. I want to make an effort not to immediately satisfy every desire I have. Also, I shall consciously renounce certain things. Besides that I want to think seriously about the meaning of my life in order to have a clear goal.

I've succeeded already in doing it only once every two or three weeks, and I hope with your advice and the help of God I can overcome it completely.

I'm very thankful to you because you are the only one with whom I can talk openly.

Yours,
Matthias

Dear Matthias,

Now that you've read the book, I want to answer both of your letters. First of all, a word of praise that you are working on your improvement with such energy and will power. I believe, though, you misunderstood the book if you think that by following the advice given you can overcome your problems from one day to the next. It will only help if you work toward a goal. On the other hand, you have already had tremendous success in an unusually short time. This is a decisive step in the direction of self-respect and self-control. Matthias, you certainly do not have to be ashamed and in no way are you abnormal.

In spite of your progress, though, I believe you have to dig a little deeper. Many things are probably just a degree more difficult for you than for others of your age. Since your sister is eleven years older, you are practically an only child, and for such children life is simply more difficult. You have to realize this very soberly and accept it as God's will. In addition, the loss of your father has intensified your loneliness. So you described yourself very accurately when you called yourself a *loner* suffering from shyness.

Masturbation for you is, I believe, an expression of your lack of contact with people. This is why it is at this point that you have to start to work. If you succeed in overcoming this difficulty in making contact with people, masturbation will soon become superfluous.

I'm enclosing a sheet of paper with suggestions on how to

improve your ability to express yourself and to respond to people. It is written in a very general way and meant for a broad spectrum of people. This is why you will be able to identify only with some of the suggestions. You have to decide for yourself what you think would be helpful for you and in a way become your own counselor.

Copy the points which strike you and then make a plan of action of the things you want to put into practice. (Send me a copy too.) "That which is not put into practice has no value" is a good saying.

The most important thing is that you enjoy working on yourself and do not feel burdened by it.

This work, however, will not automatically give you life's meaning, but it could be that slowly a new meaning will become visible, giving you a new picture of your goal in life. The more you act, the more you become active.

One cannot steer a parked car.

Yours,

W.T.

Dear Mr. Trobisch,

Many thanks for your letter and the enclosed suggestion sheet. Here's my answer and my plan of action:

1. *My difficulties:* When I am with others I have a tendency to stay in the background and wait until they take the first step. I am embarrassed when I'm forced to take the first step. This makes me confused and helpless. Maybe I don't have enough self-confidence and self-esteem.

It's true that I often have a longing for physical touching, but at the same time it turns me off.

Very often I suppress my feelings, both consciously and unconsciously.

2. *The cause of my difficulties:* Maybe I have these difficulties because I was trained never to show my feelings. Rarely

did I have the chance of learning how to express affection because this never happened in our family. I'm also afraid of being taken advantage of or of getting hurt if I open up to others.

3. *Changes I want to make:*

a. I shall try to observe how others express their feelings, especially appreciation and thankfulness. Also, when I see a good film or read a good book, I shall try to learn how the characters express their emotions.

b. When I'm supposed to meet someone, I'll try to overcome my own shyness by thinking of an honest compliment I can tell him when I see him.

c. If I feel like avoiding meeting someone, instead of running away I'll take a deep breath and go straight toward him and greet him in a friendly way.

d. Instead of avoiding all physical contact with people around me, I'll try first of all to learn to accept physical touching and then to give it myself beginning with my own family and friends.

e. I'll tell myself over and over again that it is probably much more important to others what I think of them than what they think of me.

f. I shall concentrate more on others by listening to their problems rather than sharing my own with them.

g. If I'm in a group I won't just stare into space or look down at the floor in front of me, but from time to time I'll look straight into the eyes of the others.

h. I must learn also that painful and negative feelings can bring people closer to each other. Just when I think, "Why should I burden him with it?" (and I think that very often) I'll take a deep breath and share with him what's on my heart.

This is the plan of action I've worked out so far. Please check on me after a few weeks to see if I've done it.

During Christmas vacation I went skiing. I like it so much that I forget about everything around me. Now I go skiing every other weekend as long as there's snow.

Almost every evening I meet with some of my classmates. Besides that, I'm enrolled in a dancing course which they all attend too. I hope that through these social activities I can get away from masturbation.

Sometimes I'm still afraid, but only when I come home because then I feel so lonesome.

I think I haven't yet really found the meaning of my life. On the one hand, I want to serve God, but on the other hand I dream of a good job and a motorcycle like every boy does.

Many thanks for all the trouble you've taken with me.

Yours,
Matthias

Dear Matthias,

Your letter made me very happy. You've made tremendous progress.

I agree, skiing and dancing are the best therapy for you.

Having a good job and serving God are not necessarily alternatives. Actually you can serve God in every profession. The same with your motorcycle. I had a motorcycle myself for many years and it served me well in my missionary work in Germany and Africa.

Keep on going forward! God does wonders!

Yours,
W.T.

Reflection

I debated a long time whether or not I should include Matthias's plan of action in this book. But there are so many who ask the question: How can I work on myself?

I think Matthias gives us a good example. He does not sit on the pity pot and say, "Poor me! I have no father, no brothers and sisters close to me in age, and besides that I'm in boarding school. No wonder I am as I am. This is just the way it is and no one can do anything about it."

No. Matthias works. He makes a plan and puts it into action. Once he had opened up to me in his first letter, it was like the floodgates were broken. As soon as he had the feeling that he was making progress, new joy and strength overcame him.

Many adults could learn something from this sixteen-year-old. My wife said when I read this correspondence in our family circle: "I have great respect for this young man." One of my sons added, "He really means business."

But the most interesting remark came from our youngest daughter: "Such a fellow isn't detracted by the feelings of some of us girls." She meant that in a positive way. He does not dissipate his energies with superficial love affairs, but goes straight toward his goal.

Having no father is a tremendous burden. It could be that it is even more difficult for a girl than for a boy. The correspondence with Johanna illustrates this.

"My father hates me"
10

"Why are you born if you're not loved?
. . . I was going to lose my father forever. . . . He
was cold to me—downright cold—and it was
him I loved the most. . . . Sometimes I wish I were
already experiencing menopause."
Johanna G., age 16, parents divorced

Dear Walter,

I have no idea how old you are, but I just have to write you. I
should have done it long ago. I've read your book *Love Is a
Feeling to Be Learned*. I don't remember the contents completely anymore, but I do remember that I thought it was good.
It helped me very much, and I wanted to buy it but I couldn't get
it anywhere.

I'm desperate. I don't know how to go on. Why are you born
if you're not loved? You're simply alone! Do you know what
that means? To be alone, always alone! Of course I have a
mother and a brother and sister who like me. But why have I
never received the love of my father? I love him so much. I always have loved him so much, but he hates me—and how! It
sounds really crazy to have everything (a room for myself, a
school to attend, neither hunger nor thirst) and yet be so lonesome. It's awful when there's no love. Everything inside me is a
dead stillness.

My parents have been divorced for eight years. My brother and I live with my mother. My sister is already married. Married!!! She's never had to suffer in the way that I must suffer. When she was my age she had already met her future husband and that helped her to get over the whole thing with my parents. I remember how, at that time, my girl friend's parents did not allow her to play with me because my parents were in the process of getting a divorce. She told me this on the street and I went home and cried for hours on end. A world of dreams had broken down within me.

I began then to understand that I was going to lose my father forever. It was so hard for me, even though I barely knew him. As long as I can remember I probably only met him ten times. He was cold to me—downright cold—and it was him I loved the most.

The day that girl friend talked to me, I ran home crying. I rushed into the kitchen blinded with tears and didn't see my sister until it was too late. She insisted that I tell her everything. Then she told me that she had her boyfriend and that it didn't make any difference to her what people said.

Then she said to me, "Someday you will meet a man who loves you and to whom it doesn't matter if your parents are divorced." I clung to her words. Lately, I've asked myself time and again, "What does God want from you, Johanna?" Why does he let me suffer so much? He must see that I am in anguish. All I know is that I can't stand it much longer. I shall become sick. I feel it already. Last year it was terrible. Again and again I broke down in school and had to vomit. The doctors couldn't find anything wrong with me.

But I knew what was wrong: I wanted to be loved and I wanted to love. I've tried so hard. I try to love everybody and to a certain degree I've succeeded. A lot of boys and girls come to me with their problems and cry their hearts out on my shoulder, just like I'm doing now on your shoulder (even though it's after 11:00 P.M. and my mother thinks I'm sleeping).

I've repressed my problem and I thought it would soon be over. But it didn't help. I have suffered and I still suffer in my heart. I hate myself for not being able to talk with anyone about it. Maybe I don't want to. I am two persons. I can live in such a way that no one realizes what I'm thinking. Yet I'm not happy.

Not long ago I became sixteen and I asked myself, "Doesn't God see you? Doesn't he look down upon you?" I can't remember what else I thought, but I knew one thing: God doesn't love me anymore, and he never will love me. He has forsaken me. I cried and cried. I often ask myself, "Why didn't God let my suicide attempt a year ago succeed?"

I'm so confused. Please excuse me, but I'm so mixed up. All this feeling that is boiling in me crushes everything else to pieces—simply everything. My youth is gone without my ever being happy.

I don't know whether you are the one who wrote the book *I Loved a Girl,* but you probably know about it. I am so glad for those people. But I also accuse God—yes, I do, even though my heart is broken and I'm ashamed of my words. What I really would like to do is to ask for forgiveness. Forgiveness from God the Almighty whom I love so much. But he is cold just like my father when I told him, "I love you." I don't know what God wants to do with me. A deep wound will remain in my heart my whole life. It comes from all those years when I was alone, as I still am.

My best girl friend, I love her, is from Brazil, and she has now returned to Brazil for good. She is gone, gone out of my life. I miss her very much. The little bit of life which she gave me broke again into a thousand pieces. She's twice as old as I am, but in spite of that we understood each other very deeply.

I don't know whether I can expect an answer from you or not. But through your book, I respect you a little bit because you say things as they are. From the depth of my heart I wish you and your house God's blessing.
Johanna

P.S. Thank you for everything that you do. I have a feeling that you are a pastor.

Dear Johanna,

I thank you for your letter. You guessed right. I am indeed a pastor. I'm in my fifties and I have five children, some younger and some older than you. I enclose a picture of our family so that you can get a better impression.

I think it is good that you wrote down your whole grief and pain because in this way you let it out. I listened to you attentively.

You certainly do have an especially difficult lot. When I was reading your letter and pondering your life's path, the following word from Psalm 68:19 came to my mind: "Praise the Lord, who carries our burdens day after day" (Good News Bible). In the German Bible it's translated: "God puts a burden on our shoulders, but he also helps us carry it."

One thing you must know for sure: God is not cold like your father, but he is warm. He loves you deeply, and you can never fall deeper than into his hands of love. This you can believe with all your heart even though you may not feel it. I would like to call out to you, "Johanna, fear not, only believe." *Only believe* means "to believe even though you don't see or feel anything."

However heavy your burden may be, you shouldn't give in to feeling sorry for yourself. Self-pity does not change a thing. Because God loves you, he knows exactly how much you can carry. The burden he puts on you comes out of his loving hand, and it is not one ounce heavier than your strength allows. I really believe that God has something very special in mind for you. I could imagine that he wants to train you as a real helper who is able (maybe more than I am) to aid others in the same situation—people who suffer because of the loss of their fathers and the divorce of their parents.

Evidently God has already given you a gift in this direction because you say that people come to you to cry on your shoulder. This is very unusual and extraordinary for someone at the age of sixteen. People seem to feel that you can understand them because your own suffering has matured you.

It is this gift which you must make use of and work on its development. Every gift is also a responsibility. Maybe this will be the special commission from God for your life—to help others. Therefore, you must learn to love your burden as the most precious thing which God has entrusted to you.

This will take many years of work. If you want to succeed in it, the most important thing now is that God become your Father in a very personal and concrete way. It could even be that you will be given a relationship to God much deeper than those who still have earthly fathers.

But in order for this to happen you must talk personally with your heavenly Father every day. The best time is the first thing in the morning. He wants to talk to you; and he waits for you to talk with him.

I'm enclosing a little devotional booklet, Daily Texts of the Moravian Church. In it you will find a verse from the Old Testament and a corresponding verse from the New Testament for every day. Read these words every day just as if your heavenly Father were talking to you, his daughter.

Then you should reply to him by writing down in a little notebook the answers to the following four questions:

1. In which way do these words make me thankful?
2. In which way do they correct me?
3. For what and for whom do they remind me to pray?
4. What do they mean for my activities today?

You will see that if you start your day with a talk like this then the feelings of coldness and loneliness will leave you. You will feel that your heavenly Father walks right beside you during the whole day.

Very cordially,
Your W.T.

Dear Father,

May I call you that? Because you have a daughter my age, I think it is more correct than "Dear Walter." Besides that, you really have talked to me in your letter like a father.

I cannot yet believe what you wrote in the last paragraph of your letter, but perhaps I shall learn to believe it through you.

Your letter made me glad, yet there is a sadness which overwhelms me again and again because I have to think of my physical father. It is raining and I have the feeling that each drop of rain is a tear flowing out of my innermost being. I have written a poem which I want to send to you and I have written a letter to my physical father, just for myself. I shall not mail this letter to him. No, I shall never do it but I want to tell you everything I have written to him. I feel it all again so strongly and I long so much for love. It is hard for me to wait. It is like walking through hell for me.

My father,

My father, I have loved you since early childhood, but when you realized my love for you, your hatred grew and you disliked me still more. Father, I loved you anyway in spite of all the beatings and those cold, unloving words which came from your mouth. My heart was full of hope. Yes, my heart consisted only of hope, but the way you acted just ate it all up slowly—my whole love, my hope. When I think of you now, my heart remains cold while formerly it trembled with joy.

For a long time I thought I had forgotten you completely. I thought I was indifferent toward you, that I had blotted you out of my mind. But when you called once and I heard your voice very close to my ear, everything in me was torn apart again. Like in a film, I saw again everything before me.

That time when you beat up mama, when you wanted to kill her, wanted to kill me, your cold words so infinitely far away, your cold eyes—all that I saw again in front of me. And father, in spite of that, I was happy to hear your voice. Father, from that moment on I knew I would never forget you, even though you were a stranger to me from the beginning, even though you had condemned my life to torture. Father, I love you in spite of it all.

How happy I was when I saw the loving fathers of my friends. I could observe them without envy or jealousy. But afterward, when I was alone on the street, at school, shopping, sitting on my bed at night, yes, even in the midst of a crowd of people, I felt the pain, father, which you, probably without even knowing it, have caused me for my whole life. Often I cried when I was with people, whether I stood or sat or ran, I longed so much for your love. Tears streamed down by the bucketful. I had no power over my body, and I often cried for hours at a time. I found no relief for the cruel experience ate up my ego. It was much worse than torture.

Beloved father, I have thousands of questions to ask you, but why should I ask them, for you yourself do not know the answer. Everything has already happened. If you were to read this, it would probably be all the same to you. You might want to make up for it, but this is impossible, father. What you have killed once, you cannot make come to life again. It remains dead.

A thousand questions are on the tip of my tongue, but I won't ask them. I'll never tell them to anyone and they will continue to be a great burden for me—a burden, which I will have to carry, under which I often break down and then lie on the ground, prostrate, crying and weeping.

Father, I'm still very young, but I don't know how to continue to live. I'm afraid you might come back someday to kill me and mama. You see how much I want to live and how my soul cries out for life.

Father, you don't believe there is a soul. Did you not also grow up without a mother? Excuse me! I have a question on my lips. Father, you could have given me so much of that which you missed yourself as a child. Instead you have abandoned me to a life still worse, a life with the knowledge that you hate me and that you wanted to take my life.

Father, my father, whom I love and whom I have loved from the very beginning, I do not accuse you, but you should know that my life is desperate, that I am longing, longing for love which nobody can give me because it is too late.
Johanna

Reflection
I advised Johanna to send this letter to her father, but she has not done it. Maybe it was healing enough just to be able to write it and mail it to someone.

I wish all parents who think of divorce would read it, especially all fathers. The divorce of a child's parents means that someone takes an axe and splits the child right through the middle.

To me personally the letter was an admonition to think even more seriously of my role as a father and to accept my being a father consciously and joyfully.

I was able to visit Johanna briefly. I discovered that she had faithfully followed my suggestion of a daily talk with her heavenly Father. She had filled a whole notebook with the answers to the four questions I gave her and showed it to me with pride.

After a while she wrote another letter, this time on another subject, and addressed it to my wife. I include it intentionally in this book because so many sixteen-year-old girls have difficulty with their cycles. I also think it doesn't hurt for young men to get an idea of these problems. Here is Johanna's letter.

Dear Ingrid,

I'm making myself write you. I read once more the book *My Beautiful Feeling*. It made me very sad. Originally I wanted to wait to write to you until after your trip, but I cannot wait. I simply have to spit it out.

I enjoy being a girl and by no means would I want to be a boy. But slowly I'm beginning to hate my cycle. When I was eleven I had my first period. I wasn't quite sure then what it all meant, but I felt a deep joy which I never sensed again.

This joy also satisfied my longing. It was a deep inward feeling coming from inside my body. It was like a warm surge radiating my being. I shall never forget the way my eyes looked at me from the mirror. I was happy, really happy.

At the age of fourteen I began having terrible pains with my period. At fifteen I went to see a gynecologist.

He was very gentle and prescribed a hormone treatment, each day a pill and none during menstruation. This continued for three months! The pains stopped, but I made the shocking discovery that my breasts grew considerable during this time. As a matter of fact I can't stand women with big breasts. They strike me as so obtrusive, so pushy. Therefore, it was very clear to me—no pills anymore! Naturally, I hoped that my breasts would get smaller again. When this didn't happen, I was depressed for a long time and tried to stay away from my friends. I was very inhibited.

All the things I tried at that time were really crazy. I tried to sleep on my stomach all night, and when I would wake up in the morning and discover I was lying on my back, I would be furious and put on a bra that was two sizes too small. I soon gave this up though, because my skin rebelled and I had open sores where the bra rubbed.

I still do this now and then. I'm really ashamed and angry at the doctor who changed me in such a way that I can't stand myself anymore. It was a year ago that all this happened.

And now I'm sitting here filled with fear when I think of my next menstruation. It causes me such maddening pains that I think they must already be like labor pains. Could that be—that some women have such strong pains, not just while giving birth, but also when they menstruate?

I had my last period just before a geography test. Can you imagine how I felt? It wasn't only that I couldn't concentrate— this was impossible anyway—but I simply couldn't sit still! This is the hardest thing for me because it makes the cramps worse. When I got back home that evening I cried a lot and was filled with hatred for the whole men's world. Why do we girls have to suffer, whether we want to or not, and boys always think that a woman's world is just a world of moods. I wished sometimes that at least once in his life every man would have a period with terrible pains so he could feel it in his own body. Then let's see whether he too wouldn't feel moody!

This all sounds so mean, I know. But what shall I do? I simply can't understand why for three years I had no trouble with menstruation and now there's such a change. I'd like to ask you whether there's something I can do to make the pains go away without having to stay in bed for a couple of days with a hot water bottle on my stomach. It's very embarrassing for me to know that all those around me realize what is the matter with me. Who would like to live with such a girl? I wouldn't! I'm very unhappy about it and sometimes I wish I were already experiencing menopause. I don't like to feel like a swollen-up dumpling, especially not in summer.

Please answer me!

Johanna

Dear Johanna,

Thank you so much for taking the courage to write me about this problem, which I also went through as well as my daughters. There are things you can do to help with the pains, just as a woman in labor can learn, not to fight against her contractions, but to "ride" with them.

I know a very kind and experienced gynecologist who is a good friend of ours. Since I'm just getting ready to leave on a long trip, I've asked him to answer your letter in detail. By the way, his book, *The Menstrual Cycle,* was published by W. B. Saunders Co. in Philadelphia in 1977 and has become a medical classic. He and his good wife have studied and recorded the cycle in hundreds of women for forty years now!

It may help you, Johanna, instead of being filled with fear about your next period, to say goodbye to your last one, knowing that it will never come again. It's like mountain-climbing— every step leads you closer to your goal. So take heart, lift up your eyes and discover the great adventure of being a woman!
With my love,
Ingrid Trobisch

Dear Johanna,

Ingrid Trobisch has asked me to answer your last letter. I am a gynecologist and am especially interested in the woman's development.

The pains which bother you so much are caused by your uterus. Your guess is right that they are a sort of labor pain. From other aspects also you can compare menstruation with birth. It is rather like a miscarriage because during your period, the uterus expels the nest, the lining of the womb which was prepared in case a pregnancy should take place.

Almost all young women have some discomfort during their periods—cramps, the urge to urinate and more frequent bowel movements. Some young ladies also suffer from severe colic and painful contractions. Unfortunately, we know very little about their causes.

That you had no cramps during the early years has something to do with the fact that at that time your ovaries did not yet really function. Probably no ovulation took place. Through the hormone therapy (the pills) the doctor who treated you put you artificially back into this infantile state. But this doesn't really help you because you don't want to remain a child all your life and from the point of view of nature you cannot stop growth.

The enlargement of your breasts has possibly been caused by the doctor's treatment, but it could also be your natural development. Maybe you are exaggerating a little bit because as a girl you feel somehow exposed because of your breasts, and also your breasts remind you of your next menstruation. Just look once at your classmates' breast measurements. Maybe you will find some of them with even larger breasts.

Here are a few practical suggestions:

1. Take an active part in physical education, at least once a week in a group and every evening do some exercises before you go to bed. It would be good if you could take an intensive course in women's rhythmic gymnastics. Ride a bicycle every day for half an hour, preferably uphill.

2. Diet: Take *no* weight-reducing pills. Eat a lot of proteins (lean meat, liver, fish, cheese, cottage cheese and other milk products). Drink a lot of warm liquids (milk, mint tea, herb tea with lemon juice and as little sugar as possible). Stay away from coffee and black tea. Eat a lot of fruit, fresh vegetables and salads. Be careful to eat few fats, sweets, chocolate, starchy foods, bread and baked goods.

3. During the days before your period go to bed early, keeping your head at a lower level than your hips and legs. Before your period begins put a warm, damp bath towel on your stomach covered with a warm water bottle while you sleep.

4. Clothing: Keep your feet, legs and pelvic region very warm before your period. Warm underclothes are very important. Don't wear shoes that are too tight, boots or tight belts. Don't ride on motorbikes.

5. Take some pain-killing medicine only if it's really necessary.

Did Mrs. Trobisch write to you about taking your waking temperature?

If you take your temperature every morning before getting up, you can see that it rises a little bit during the time of ovulation when the egg leaves the ovary. About two weeks later, shortly before menstruation, it goes down again. This is why taking your temperature can help you to prepare for your period.

That's enough for today. Write if you have questions.
With all good wishes,
Yours,
Rudolf F. Vollman

Dear Dr. Vollman,

Today I got up courage to write to you because the difficulties with my period are getting worse.

But first of all I want to thank you from the depths of my heart for your letter. I am very glad that I can come to you with these problems and that you give me such valuable advice.

During summer vacation I rode my bike a lot and was also very involved in sports. Shortly before I got my period I kept myself warm and elevated my hips with a pillow under them.

By taking my waking temperature I could tell just when menstruation would begin. This was one of the most beautiful experiences I had during the summer. I had no pains, or only very weak ones that didn't interfere with my daily activities.

But now I still have a question which is embarrassing to me because I don't know if it's a stupid question.

I hope you understand me. During the first days of my period when the bleeding is very strong, there are blood clumps or clots which then disappear the third or fourth day. When they are expelled I feel pressure from inside which is sometimes very painful. I've tried several things to make them milder, but I found it's best if I just stand still and wait until it's over. It's very uncomfortable and sometimes I almost feel like fainting. Perhaps you could write to me about this. I'm very happy that I can write to you.
Johanna

Dear Johanna,

I just received your letter and will answer it immediately.

Isn't it interesting that you can learn how your body functions by taking your waking temperature?

Menstruation is not just bleeding. On the contrary, the bleeding is actually a side effect. After ovulation, the inner lining of the uterus is prepared for a possible pregnancy. The lining grows, becomes thicker and is filled with special nutrients. If no conception has taken place, these preparations are superfluous. When the body realizes this, the temperature drops and the lining is expelled. Then you see these blood clumps which are a part of the nest. Through this process a small wound is caused inside the uterus which bleeds and you have your period. The expulsion is caused by the periodic contractions of the uterus, very similar to the labor contractions at the beginning of the birth process.

With friendly greetings,
Rudolf F. Vollman

Reflection

I learned from the correspondence between Johanna and Dr. Vollman that the advice to live consciously with and in a positive attitude toward her cycle is often given to a girl much too late. We may think that taking the waking temperature is only useful for married couples planning a family.

But sixteen is probably the right age to begin doing this—for certain girls even earlier. In any case, it helps a woman accept herself and in this way it is useful even if she does not marry. If she does, it's one of the best preparations for married life.

Living consciously with her cycle helped Johanna to accept herself as a girl. This even helped her cramps and lessened her pain, as she confirmed later on.

There is one theme from her first letter we have not yet touched. She commented on the departure of her girl friend, who went back to Brazil, with these words: "The little bit of life which she gave me broke again into a thousand pieces."

A lot of things would certainly have been easier for Johanna if her girl friend could have been with her. Over and over again I have pointed out the importance of having a friend of the same sex.

This will be the main topic in the next two letter exchanges.

"In my home there's always fighting"
11

"When I'm not with my friend, I feel
something like a very strong longing. . . . There's
always fighting at my home. I'd like to
move out and live with my friend. . . . What is the
difference between wet dreams and
masturbation?"
Ullrich S., age 16, high-school student

Dear Sir,

I'm writing to you because I have a lot of questions and believe that you can best answer them.

My problem is masturbation. I've talked to a lot of people about it, but I still hang onto it.

I'm sixteen. I've been a Christian for some years now, and I'm an active church member.

Maybe I'm in the process of solving my problem. In any case I've learned that I can't solve it all at once. Now I try to solve it step by step. If I do it only every third day, that's progress for me. But I don't yet see a real goal.

I'm practically an only child even though I have two brothers, one thirty-one and the other twenty-six. I have very little contact with them. I play the guitar and go to high school.

It would be my greatest desire to have a brother who's a little bit older or younger than I. Then I could room with him. (I have a room by myself.) I have a friend who's a Christian too. I'm with him very often. Once in a while I stay overnight with him or he with me. And this brings up my first question.

I've read your book *My Beautiful Feeling*. There you write about three phases everyone goes through during adolescence. The second phase is characterized by deep friendships between members of the same sex. What is meant by "signs of affection"? Why do they stop before sexual expression?

And how about feelings? I do feel something for my friend. When I'm not with my friend, I feel something like a very strong longing. Is this normal?

Nine months ago I had the same feeling about someone else, but then it disappeared. I'm afraid that this will happen again with my friend—that this feeling will vanish after a few months.

There's always fighting at my home. My parents fight very often. I'd like to move out and live with my friend, but this is not possible. Would it be good if we lived together? Could we become too attached to each other? By the way, he's seventeen and has a girl friend. Are my feelings toward him normal?

Recently, I read a book which said that wet dreams are quite normal. It also said that sexual tensions are natural and that through the ejaculation during sleep, tension is released—but what is the difference between wet dreams and masturbation?

Maybe the whole thing has something to do with my nickname. Two years ago we played a skit at a retreat. I had to play a character who was very stupid. Since then everyone calls me Snooky. And somehow my last two years are connected with this nickname. If someone calls me Snooky, I get the feeling that I'm not really accepted as a person. I can't stand the name.

I hope I will soon receive an answer from you.

Yours,
Ullrich

Dear Ullrich,

Thank you for your letter. Let me begin with your questions

concerning the difference between wet dreams and masturbation. A wet dream is an ejaculation of seminal fluid which happens involuntarily at night during sleep. Masturbation is a conscious action which involves the will.

In our book *My Beautiful Feeling,* you read that everyone has to go through three phases during adolescence. The first phase is called the autoerotic phase in which feelings of love are still directed toward oneself. Masturbation is a physical expression of this phase. Therefore when you masturbate, it means you are still at least partially in this phase.

There is no reason to worry a lot about it as long as you are working on overcoming it. If you have to do it only every third day, that is progress for you. Gradually you will grow out of it and look on it as something childish and unsatisfactory. You should slowly be able to lengthen the intervals until it stops completely and you are strong enough to stand up under tension without having to seek release immediately.

Your guitar can be of great help to you in this respect. Play it as often as you like.

The second phase in this process of maturing is the homoerotic phase. It simply means that the ego is mature enough to build a bridge to another person, but it is not yet strong enough to establish a lasting relationship with the opposite sex.

This will be possible only in the heteroerotic phase. Then the ego is strong enough to overcome the fear of the otherliness of another person, and you are able to love someone of the other sex.

For the time being, however, until this maturity has been reached, a compromise is made during the second phase. Our love feelings turn toward someone who is different, yet still as much as possible like ourselves. In other words, we turn toward someone of the same sex. This is why during the second phase very deep friendships between two girls or between two boys take place.

This is what you now experience with your friend. You see,

it's impossible to make a clear-cut separation between the first and second phase. There is a certain overlapping. Longing for your friend means that you have to a certain extent entered the second stage.

Such a deep friendship between two boys your age is not only normal, it's also healthy and good. You learn to deal with love feelings and to enjoy them without transforming them into sexual actions. If you learn how to do this now with a friend of your own sex, it will be less difficult later on to keep this limit when you enter into a relationship with a girl.

You don't need to be afraid of physical touching. There's nothing wrong with putting your arm around the shoulders of your friend. This won't cause too strong an attachment.

I'm sure what you're afraid of when you think of this is homosexuality. This danger is indeed present, but only when you indulge in sexual activities, such as mutual masturbation. Then it would indeed be possible for you to get stuck in the second stage so that you will not mature into the third stage and be able to enter into a relationship with a girl. In order not to cross over this fine borderline, I think it would be better not to move into the same room as your friend and, if you visit him, not to sleep in the same bed.

I can well understand that you sometimes feel lonesome in your room, but you should also learn to enjoy being alone. Many boys would like to have a room to themselves, but they can't. You have to learn two things in life: how to live alone with yourself and how to live together with someone else. The longing you experience when you are alone makes fellowship, being together, something precious.

Naturally, the feelings you have now will pass. You must be prepared for the fact that when you are eighteen you will think back on the feelings you have now and simply shake your head at your old problems. More and more you will feel attracted to girls. Living through these confused feelings is a painful but also a positive experience. It means that you are growing out of the homoerotic phase into the heteroerotic phase, but it does not mean that you should not enjoy what you are now experiencing and all that is given to you.

From your nickname you can learn who you do not want to be. This is also valuable. It's only in this way that you can learn who you are, Ullrich.

I greet you very cordially.

Your W.T.

Reflection

I hope that Ullrich's letter will bring relief to many who have similar feelings, but who do not want to admit it for fear of being thought homosexual. However, I also hope that my answer will help many to respect the borderline between two members of the same sex.

It could be that some of those who read this book have already made mistakes in this respect. To them I would like to recommend the next exchange of letters and assure them that even then not all is lost.

Chapter twelve deals with two girls who have crossed the borderline.

They have the same lot as Ullrich, homes where there is no harmony in the family. Martina is an unwanted child whose mother doesn't hesitate to let her know it. Gerda's mother is a businesswoman who has four children and neither the time nor patience to establish a warm relationship with her daughter.

None of us is a hundred-per-cent male or a hundred-per-cent female. In every man there's also something feminine and in every woman there's something masculine. Otherwise, the sexes could not understand each other. The question is, what is the dominant factor? In men it should be the masculine and in women the feminine factor.

This balance is reached when the young boy can identify with his father and the girl with her mother. If for one reason or the other this process of identification does not or cannot take place, the danger of homosexuality is present. When the boy identifies with his mother, the feminine becomes the dominant factor, and he looks for a man as his partner. On the other hand, if a girl identifies with her father, the masculine becomes the dominant factor in her personality, and she will look for a woman as a partner.

I suppose that something like this must have happened with Martina and Gerda when they entered into a deep friendship with each other. When this friendship began to find sexual expression they became worried and wrote to me.

"All of a sudden we helped each other"
12

---

*"All of a sudden we helped each other get
rid of our tension. . . . In the end we were
very ashamed of ourselves. Both of us know we
will ruin our friendship slowly but surely."*
Martina S., age 17   Gerda D., age 18

Dear Mr. Trobisch,

We—Martina, seventeen and Gerda, eighteen—have read
your book *My Beautiful Feeling.* We have been good friends
for some months now and understand each other very well.
We have a mutual problem and agree that we need a third person to help us find a way out. Separately, without talking it over
with each other, we both thought of you.

Would you perhaps have time to deal with our problem? Can
we be sure that you will not share it with anyone else except
your wife?
Many greetings,
Martina and Gerda

Dear Martina and Gerda,

Of course you can write to me about your problem. You can
also be assured that your letters will be treated confidentially

and that no one else will read them. [Gerda and Martina later gave me permission to publish their letters.]
With cordial greetings,
Your W.T.

Dear Mr. Trobisch,

Gerda and I believe it would be better to write you separately. I have known Gerda now for six months, and I liked her from the moment I saw her. I felt she understood me as no one else ever had before. I could tell her everything that came to my mind, and whenever I needed her she had time for me.

This had never happened before in my life. I only had a mother, and she had to go to work so she never had time for me. Besides that I was a burden to her. Because of me she couldn't work where she really wanted to work. I guess my mother would have preferred it if I had never been born. But she couldn't change things. She had been raped. She has often told me and made me feel unwanted.

That's why I was very happy when I could leave home. Here at the hotel where I'm working I found a person to love. Gerda has given me her undivided love, something I never experienced before. I trust her completely. Once I told her of something which had burdened me for almost ten years. I was afraid of her reaction, but she understood me. After that my love grew still deeper.

When I asked her whether there was anything she had not told me, instead of an answer she showed me a magazine article about masturbation. After that my love for her grew still deeper.

I was neither surprised nor shocked. When she came back to my room, I took her in my arms and told her that I loved her just as much as before and that I would try to help her.

Since then I've slept with her once in a while. It was so beautiful to lie in bed and talk together and touch each other. Is this bad? Once when we slept together in the same bed, I could feel that Gerda was aroused. She didn't want to masturbate in my presence, but the urge was so strong that she finally did it.

I didn't know what to do. I was also aroused, but I could not find release in Gerda's presence. I was too ashamed and later on Gerda told me that she also had been ashamed.

Now I come to the heart of the problem. One day—I don't know anymore when it was or how it happened—we laid together in bed and were both aroused.

All of a sudden we helped each other get rid of our tension. I really didn't know what I was doing. It was only afterward that we realized it. Then it happened again and again. We couldn't stop. In the end we were very ashamed of ourselves.

Both of us know we will ruin our friendship slowly but surely. It happens to us now almost every day.

We've already decided to pray. But we often forget or think there will be time for it later on. I tell myself again and again that it has to stop, but before I realize it, it has happened again.

I don't know any way out. I don't want to give up this friendship. It is too precious for me. Many thanks for helping us.
Your Martina

Dear Mr. Trobisch,

Finally I—the friend of Martina—have been able to bring myself to write to you. I wanted to do it all the time, but I just couldn't make myself. I was too ashamed to put into words the problem we have. I didn't want to face it, and above all I was afraid my parents would hear about it.

I'm glad that Martina had the courage to take the risk and write you. I believe that with your help we can solve the problem.

I come from a home where both parents are Christians and try to do God's will. What depresses me is the hectic rush at home because we run a shop. My mother, a businesswoman with four children, is overburdened and often has no patience.

School did not challenge me enough, and I often had the impression that my life was unfulfilled and without joy or meaning. I lost good friends again and again. I often wept at home, and sometimes I didn't even want to live anymore.

Then I decided to leave home and work in a hotel. Here I changed my whole attitude toward life. I could be young, cheerful and have no worries. The reason for this, besides having a good job which challenged me, was my friendship with Martina, a curly-headed brunette with a lot of personality, who won my heart immediately. We had a wonderful summer and experienced a lot of happiness being together which neither of us had ever known before.

One day we told each other we loved one another. We shared with each other just what this love meant. It was so wonderful, and yet sometimes I thought, are girls allowed to express these feelings to each other and even to touch each other?

What happened then Martina has written to you. It is hard for me to put it into words. I just want to add that during the time when it started we talked a lot about sexual things and shared our thoughts and opinions. I believe we talked too much about it and that aroused our imaginations.

It is also important to mention that we have learned to pray together. This makes me happy.

My letter is rather confused, but perhaps you can understand it just the same.

Many greetings and again thank you!
Gerda

Dear Martina and Gerda,

It's good that you have written. A special word of praise goes to Martina that she overcame her feeling of shame and dared to write such an open and concrete letter.

Just let me tell you one thing in advance. The feelings of shame and embarrassment which both of you experience very strongly are your greatest and best guides. They are very healthy feelings which you should not suppress. Without doubt they tell you that you have started to move along the wrong path and that you have to stop and turn around.

It is not yet too late. Therefore, there is no need to worry. But it's very necessary that you change your behavior as soon as possible, otherwise you may get in a rut and it will be very difficult to get out of it later on. It could make marriage for you very hard if not impossible.

From my book *My Beautiful Feeling,* you know that the development of human sexuality undergoes three phases. The second phase is the homoerotic phase when deep boy-boy and girl-girl friendships grow.

Both of you are experiencing this second phase now, which in itself is healthy and good. The fact that you feel these things so strongly and intensely has something to do with your family situation. Martina has no father and Gerda doesn't mention hers. Both of you have difficult relationships with your mothers.

Evidently, you try to replace the love you were deprived of at home by each other. This in itself is not wrong. I can well understand how happy it makes you. Of course, you are allowed to express your feelings for each other.

But you crossed a boundary by indulging in sexual activities. At that point, your consciences reacted immediately and you were warned by your feelings of shame.

No damage has been done yet. But if you continue on this road you could become fixated by the attraction of the same sex and this would be hard to change later on. Through this intimate sex play with each other, this dependence on one another would finally ruin your friendship. Martina has rightly foreseen this danger.

Every repetition of sexual action in this way will increase this fixation. As I said before, you get into a rut that will be hard to get out of later on. It could become such an ingrained habit that you won't be able later on to bridge the gap to the other sex and you will become homosexual, or lesbian, as one calls it when women are involved.

Now you may be shocked. But I had to use the word which you probably are afraid to say. Once again, I don't think that you have yet reached this point. You certainly are not lesbian. Don't worry about it. But the danger is there if you keep going in the wrong direction.

My advice to you is to be hard on yourselves and consequently on each other. By no means should you sleep in the same bed anymore, possibly not even in the same room, so that you do not have to undress in front of each other. Also, for the time being I would advise you to refrain from any physical touching. There are so many other ways of expressing tenderness and love—through a gesture, a look, a smile, a word, a letter, a little gift, and certainly through prayer.

Help each other to avoid compromise. You will see that in this way your friendship will actually grow deeper and you will lose nothing.

It is good that you can pray together. It will give you the strength you need to obey God's commandments. I shall also pray for you.

Yours,

W.T.

Dear Mr. Trobisch,

Thank you very much for your letter which we had looked forward to with great eagerness because we didn't know which way to turn. It has always been clear to both of us that this was the wrong way for a friendship to go, but we could not free ourselves from it. Every time it happened, we felt great remorse and were completely desperate.

We had often wondered whether we were homosexual, but we could not resolve the question. Sometimes we didn't even dare to admit to each other we thought about it. We are grateful that you have made us conscious of it.

We made the following decision: From now on, each of us will spend the night in her own room. We have limited our caresses to a hug and stroking each other's cheeks. We believe that we can be responsible for this because this has never led us into temptation. We will refrain from kissing, because that was sometimes the cause. It is hard for us, but we want it this way.

We thank you for your patience and for your prayers.
Your Martina and Gerda

Reflection
Martina and Gerda have kept their word. They are now women of nineteen and twenty. We are still in contact with them. Both are developing into very normal young ladies. At present they work at different places. Each one has a boyfriend, and this fact gives them both an affirmation of their femininity. This in turn helps them very much to accept themselves as women, since neither Martina nor Gerda received this affirmation as a child from her father.

Girls are especially in danger when two things coincide in their lives: a cold mother and an unexpressive father who does not show them that they are lovable as "little women." Parents often do not realize that they themselves put their children in danger when they could save them from danger so easily.

Martina and Gerda had the courage to write a letter. I am disturbed when I think of the many others—boys as well as girls —who are in a similar situation and who keep silent. Therefore, I'm especially thankful to Martina and Gerda that they gave permission to publish their letters.

What I like best about them is the fact that they themselves drew the boundary lines. They do the same thing now with their boyfriends. It seems to me that this is easier for them now, because they practiced it with each other before.

The setting of limits is also the topic of the next correspondence, this time with a boy.

"Is Napoleon the cause of the trouble?"
13

*"Formerly I was a biblical Christian, but
for some time now I have been unfaithful. . . .
There are times when I would like to break
up with her because something is fishy. Then
I ask myself whether the 'absolute' is the
cause of the trouble or the 'Napoleon.' "*
Michael B., age 16, high-school student

Dear Mr. Trobisch,

I recently started to read your books. They are tremendous. But I have to explain something to you before I begin with the main topic of my letter.

I'm sixteen and formerly I was a biblical Christian, but for some time now I have been unfaithful.

For ten weeks and five days I have had a really nice girl friend. I like her very much and she likes me too. We often are together, and then it is not only the usual kissing, but we also talk with each other about problems, even about problems you deal with in your books. You could say that we have a fabulous friendship.

Here is my problem: As I just mentioned I like Susi very much. But there are times when I would like to break up with her because something is fishy. Then I ask myself whether the "absolute" is the cause of the trouble or the "Napoleon."

(*Absolute* means my hand on her most intimate area. *Napoleon* means my hand on her breast.)

It happens very rarely because she does not permit it. She says: "Only when I'm psychologically down do I need this kind of a lift—otherwise not." That's why it doesn't happen often.

Sometimes I think of breaking up with her after I have called her. We talk sometimes for a whole hour on the telephone. That makes me disgusted.

However, I'm unable to break up with her because when she's with me again I feel very happy and forget everything. That's the way it is with me and my Susi.

Now I've burdened you with my problem and I hope that you can give me advice.

Your Michael

P.S. I am cold (Rev. 3:16).

Dear Michael,

Thanks a lot for your letter. In general, I must say that our feelings of liking and disliking are always going up and down.

Fortunately, love is not based only on feelings, but to a certain degree also on will. It is a sober act of will which decides to love a person at any price, in every situation and for a whole lifetime, without paying any attention to the ups and downs of feelings.

Both of you, however, are still too young for this decision. I don't believe that you can make it before you are twenty or twenty-one—a few years later is still better.

The conflict in your relationship with Susi is caused by the fact that you express your affection for each other in the wrong way. These intimate caresses such as you describe are simply more than your relationship can take at the moment. I think you are right when you say you have the feeling that something is fishy. You must listen to this feeling. It's a good and healthy feeling.

I think it's very dangerous to put yourself in the role of being Susi's psychotherapist when she's down. You don't help her at all this way. All this touching increases your desire for something more, and if you grant it, your desires are increased still more, and it will be hard to put the brakes on. Maybe Susi will even be tempted to be dishonest to herself and to be "down" more often than she really is, so that she can be comforted in this way.

I believe you can help her much more if you refuse this wrong kind of comfort and put your foot down. She will certainly respect you more and feel more secure in your presence. I would shorten those long telephone calls too. They do not help her.

I think you have to learn to stick up for what you feel is right. If I were you, I would ask myself whether the voice of God is speaking when again and again you feel this desire to break up. I think you would respect yourself and love yourself much more if you would be guided more by God than by Susi and do what you feel is right. Certainly you could succeed in having a "fabulous friendship" more with a boy right now than with a girl.

Your deepest problem, though, seems to be that you have lost your faith. I can't help but believe that this fact affects your relationship with Susi.

The crossing over of the boundary which you and Susi have set for yourselves seems to have the consequence that not only is something fishy between you and Susi, but also between you and God.

Here the "absolute" is the cause of the trouble—but in a different sense than you use the word. Susi has become more important to you than God. God, however, is a jealous God. He wants to be the absolute—the most important thing—in your life. Either you belong to him completely or you do not belong to him at all. St. Augustine has said; "He who loves not God above all, loves not God at all."

Maybe breaking up with Susi is the way to give God again the place in your life which belongs to him. And maybe this is also the greatest help for Susi to learn to deal with her "downs" in a

constructive way. Just think about it!
I greet you very cordially,
Your W.T.

Reflection

Michael is a typical young man. He counts weeks and days and I'm quite sure that the intimate caresses are more important to him than "talking over problems."

Yet he has not lost his fine sensitivity. He feels immediately when something is fishy. Also, he knows when his personal faith has come into conflict with his actions. I have a high respect for him because he does not compromise, but recognizes the consequences of his actions. He doesn't consider himself a Christian anymore.

On the other hand, he does not have the strength to change his attitudes and free himself.

I don't know whether my answer has helped him. Was it too hard and self-righteous? Could this be the reason he never answered?

We just have to let it stand. But one thing is clear: a great deal depends on how physical touching is integrated into the relationship between boys and girls—even the fate of that relationship!

The following correspondence puts light on the same problem from the point of view of a girl.

"His kisses became more and more impetuous"
14

"It was completely dark in the room. . . .
All of a sudden he pulled down the zipper of
my jeans. . . . I really got frightened."
Gabi R., age 15   boyfriend, age 16

Dear Sir,

I'm writing you because I do not know in whom else I can confide. After having read your book *Love Is a Feeling to Be Learned,* I thought you could help me understand my problems.

I'm fifteen and I have a sixteen-year-old boyfriend. We've known each other for more than two months now and we understand each other well. My parents have just as little against him as his have against me.

I must tell you that I have never had a boyfriend before who was older than I. With all the others so far I was just a good pal.

But it is different with my present friend. The other evening when I was alone with him at his home, we sat in his room and talked. The light was out, and it was completely dark in the room. All of a sudden he started to kiss me. He got more and more impetuous. Then he slipped his hand under my pullover. I just let it happen and even found it pleasant.

All of a sudden he pulled down the zipper of my jeans. A fellow had never tried that before. I pushed him away and told him to leave me in peace. I really got frightened. He tried to calm me down and pulled the zipper up again.

I think he wanted to start petting, but since I've never done that with a guy, I don't know what to do nor how it should be done. I don't think you can get pregnant through petting. I would like to avoid that if possible.

Please give me advice!
With friendly greetings,
Gabi

P.S. You can send your answer to my home address. No trouble.

Dear Gabi,

Thank you for your letter and the confidence you showed by sharing with me. It's good that you wrote immediately, before you went any further. I only hope my answer reaches you before it is too late. I would like to explain to you what happens during petting. I'm not doing it so you can try it out, but in order that you do not try it out because you are curious.

Usually by *petting* one means the mutual manipulation of the genital organs. For the male partner this usually results in an ejaculation which gives him some release, but is not really satisfying for him. It is even less so for the female partner.

Actually, petting is meant to be a prelude to the sexual union in marriage. If this union does not take place, tension is created with which it is difficult to cope. It really does not pay.

Normally, one cannot get pregnant by petting. Yet it is not impossible, for in one single seminal ejaculation there can be as many as 500,000,000 sperm. One of them, if it gets into the vagina, is enough to fertilize an ovum. If you think of the physical closeness and excitement, you can see why this happens more often than you might first imagine.

Furthermore, a lot of young people overestimate their power of resistance. They might intend only to pet, but then are unable to stop and end up having intercourse. Don't even try to see if you can put on the brakes in this way!

You're not a candy bar to be nibbled on. Don't put yourself in this role. Later on you will feel ashamed when you become engaged to someone who will be yours all your life.

By the way I want to praise you because you pushed him away. Your healthy feelings of embarrassment and shame instinctively caused this reaction. They are your guardian angels. Let yourself be guided by these voices within and be wary of those who ridicule these feelings of embarrassment and shame by calling them unnatural or neurotic!

You saw how your boyfriend respected it immediately when you valiantly defended your rights. Most fellows deeply long in their hearts for the girl to resist them. You don't lose anything by setting these limits. On the contrary, you rise in their respect. If someone breaks up with you because you stand up to him, don't shed any tears. He's not worthy of them.

You know, though, if I were in your place, I would put up my lines of defense much earlier rather than at the very last moment. You have described the steps exactly—being alone in a room, then darkness, kissing, lying down together, finally undressing and then the next step would have been intimate touching.

At the latest you should draw the line before you lie down together or even before this impetuous kissing. There's kissing, and then there's kissing. A kiss as a light touch on the forehead or the cheek can be an expression of deep-felt tenderness—just like a ray of sunshine coming through a window. But if it becomes "impetuous" and stormy, then I would ring the warning bells too early rather than too late.

Yes, even though I run the risk of being taken as hopelessly old-fashioned, I think you should be careful about being in a room alone with your friend. Believe me, you will have much more joy if you do something with others, and then you can talk about this shared experience. If you are alone in a room, then it should not be for too long and not in the dark.

You see it takes a little bit of intelligence if you want to avoid being trapped. Show this letter to your friend and talk it over with him! From his reaction you will see whether or not he is truly a "friend."

By the way, I'm glad I can write to your home address and that I don't need to use the address of a third person, as sometimes happens in the case of other correspondents your age. This shows me that your parents respect the privacy of your mail. I also see that what your parents think about your friend and what his parents think about you means something to you. Don't let them lose confidence in you.

If you had a sixteen-year-old daughter, you would want to trust her too, wouldn't you?
Cordially yours,
W.T.

Dear Sir,

I hope you still remember me. In my last letter I wrote about my friend. In this letter I'm going to write about my parents.

But before I do that I would like to thank you for your letter. It was an eye opener for me. I had a long talk with my friend after I got it. He also sees our friendship now in the right perspective. Of course, we still kiss each other and we think that if we are still going together next year we should perhaps think of getting engaged. We love each other more than anyone else, but in spite of this we want to wait until marriage.

But now about my new problem with my parents: We are slowly drifting apart. My big sister, who's twenty-four, left home a long time ago. She's a university student and my father has to support her. This puts a great burden on him. Often he's in a bad mood and sometimes my mother and I suffer because of it.

My father is fifty-three and my mother is fifty. If you saw our modern home and our whole way of life, you would think they were much younger.

They have very few friends. My mother doesn't like to have visitors nor go visiting—it's embarrassing for her. Neither do they belong to any groups or clubs. So in the late afternoon they just sit around and are edgy; in the evening they watch TV. They have a real TV-marriage.

Maybe this is the reason why they want to have me around all the time. I'm a high-school sophomore. When I've finished my homework or studied for a test and then want to go visit my friend, they always say, "Every day you run around. All right, but if you get bad grades, you'll have to break up. Your school work must not suffer."

But I do all I can to get good grades. I'm above average in my class and my grades are good enough. I just can't see why I must break up with my friend because of my school work.

On Monday, Tuesday and Wednesday I'm not allowed to see him and on the other days I have to come home early. If my parents had other interests and contacts with people, it would ease the situation. But how can they find them? I would like very much to help them. But how? Also, they should gradually begin to treat me as a grown-up. I would be very happy if you could send me some suggestions soon.
With friendly greetings,
Your Gabi

Dear Gabi,

I was very happy to hear from you again. I was especially happy that you accepted my advice and backtracked as far as intimacies go. Congratulations! It is not everyone who is able to do that. But I think that even eighteen is still too early for an engagement. Between eighteen and twenty-one you will still change very much—so will your friend. That's why I would discourage you from making such far-reaching decisions before that age.

Early marriages are one of the reasons why there are so many divorces. Just imagine being twenty-two and already having two children. It would be easy for you to look on them as disturbing factors in your life that keep you tied down. Maybe you would tell yourself, "This is how it will be for the next fifteen years of my life," and you could become very depressed.

If, on the other hand, you have already lived your own life, learned a profession and practiced it, then a crisis of this kind may be avoided. You would be a more mature mother for your children, and you could enjoy in a completely new way the challenge of being a homemaker with all of its creative possibilities.

Your parents probably foresee these things, and this is why they try to put on the brakes a little bit. I'm sure they are also fearful that you might sleep with your boyfriend, and you know yourself how close you were to that. I wonder if you could simply show your parents our correspondence and talk with them about it. Maybe this would increase their confidence in you, and they would give you more freedom.

You look at your parents' marriage very critically. Perhaps it would ease the situation if you would take the initiative and plan something you could do together over a weekend.

On the other hand, you cannot be your parents' marriage counselor, and you have to accept them simply as they are. One thing is certain, they need a lot of love and praise. You should use every opportunity to show them your gratefulness and love. Maybe as a Christmas present you could give them a game they could play together. Or do you know another couple in their age group who could visit them from time to time?

You seem to be a very fine girl, and I hope to make your acquaintance some day.

With very warm greetings,
Your W.T.

Reflection

What moved me the most about the correspondence with Gabi was the role of her parents. Certainly they are good, caring and loving people who want the very best for their child.

But do they have any idea what is happening in their daughter's mind? Do they realize that Gabi sees through the emptiness of their marriage? Do they know how much she suffers because she is supposed to replace their own lack of companionship?

As is the case with so many parents, they believe that raising children means watching over and controlling them. How much more helpful it would be for their daughter if they would have a good talk with her to explain their reasons for strict rules and concern. At the same time, Gabi seems to be in need of simple information, as her question concerning petting shows. Nowadays it is certainly the responsibility of parents to talk to their fifteen-year-old daughter about these things.

The greatest protection for a child is not in control, but in giving one's confidence completely to the child.

The attitude of Gabi's boyfriend impresses me. Frankly, I had not anticipated that he would react this way.

In spite of many pessimistic prognoses, I believe there are many young men today who can sensitively distinguish those things which help a relationship to develop and those which make it a dead-end road.

The following letter from a reticent young man underlines this again. For those who are able to read between the lines, it is a very precious letter.

"She is too precious for a flirt"
15

"Brigitta is too precious to me for just a flirt. . . . If I were made of wax I certainly would have melted."
Fritz H., age 17, tradesman

Dear Mr. Trobisch,

For two years now I've been in love with a girl from my Christian youth group, but I still would like to wait until I'm eighteen in order to be sure that my love for her is real and God's will for me.

At the moment I'm hospitalized because I had an accident with my motorcycle. Brigitta writes me every week.

When I was still in good health, I noticed often how she looked at me. Of course I did the same. But when she visited me once in the hospital, she looked at me in such a way that if I were made of wax I certainly would have melted.

I realize more and more that when I leave the hospital the moment will have come for a frank talk.

But this is my problem: There are days when if she were with me I could just squeeze her for joy. Then again there are other times when I doubt my love for her.

It could be that this up and down of feelings is normal for my age, but I would like to have your advice because Brigitta is too precious to me for just a flirt.

I hope you understand me and can help me a little bit.

Yours,
Fritz

Dear Fritz,

Thank you for your direct question. I have to admire the fact that you were able to keep the feelings you had for a girl in your heart for two years, knowing that they weren't one-sided, yet still silently and patiently waiting for certainty.

You've probably sensed that even one word said too early and too directly can destroy the magic and that a gesture made too soon can squash something very, very fragile. Therefore, it is good that you resisted the impulse to squeeze Brigitta for joy. Not only would you have squashed her, but also with her your joy. For me there is no doubt that just because you both held back, your relationship was deepened.

Yes, it is normal that your feelings go up and down. It's not only true at your age, but at every age. This will lessen once you have talked frankly with each other.

I agree with you that the time has now come for such an open talk. I could imagine that Brigitta is even more in doubt about your feelings than about her own. Very often the girl is sure about her feelings sooner than the boy.

When you talk to her, tell her candidly the reasons for your reticence—that she is too precious, far too precious for you just to flirt with her.

God bless you and guide you both when you have your talk together.

Your W.T.

Reflection
I intentionally included the letter of Fritz between the letters of

Gabi and the next correspondence in order to show the contrast in the conduct of the girls.

I do not know much about Brigitta, but it would not surprise me to learn that she had a family in which she felt sheltered and protected. Evidently, Beate, the next writer, did not have this experience. Just how this lack has affected her is expressed in this letter.

"I was always looking for my place"
16

*"My mother raised me in such a way that
I was made to think my sex organs were
something bad.... When I was thirteen I
slept with a boy for the first time....
Somehow I was always looking for my place,
for love and tenderness."*
Beate K., age 16, high-school student

Dear Mr. and Mrs. Trobisch,

I just finished reading your book *My Beautiful Feeling* for the
second time. I'm sixteen and repeating the sophomore year at
my high school.

I'm afraid this will be a long letter because at present I have
some other problems besides masturbation.

My mother has been a Christian for about seven years, but
unfortunately this has not affected her character very much.
She loses her temper very quickly, but she can also quickly forget she has been angry. My mother raised me in such a way
that I was made to think my sex organs were something bad.

When I was five or six, I played doctor with other children.
As we played we discovered the difference in our genital organs.
My mother wanted to take me to a psychiatrist and scolded me
for doing such a thing. But this only made me more curious.

When I was thirteen I slept with a boy for the first time. I
didn't like him very much, but I wanted to know whether what

I had read in books about intercourse was true and whether the feeling of orgasm was really as beautiful as it was described as being.

You will probably be shocked, but I will write very frankly. Writing is easier for me than talking with someone. For a while I met this boy frequently, but mostly we just petted.

When I was fourteen, I came home from a walk one day, and when my mother opened the door she was pale as death. She said, "Come with me to your room." In my room she opened the drawer where I kept the contraceptives and similar things.

She said I was just like a prostitute, took a bamboo stick which she hadn't used since I was five years old, and punished me until I thought I wouldn't survive.

Then she sent me to church all the time and didn't let me out of her sight. My father didn't say a word about the whole thing. (I have no relationship with him. He's an excellent father for small children. But he's simply not capable of raising teenagers.)

After that I had three other boyfriends. I petted with them more times than I can count, and once I had intercourse. The last one broke up with me three days after we had slept together. That was quite a shock for me.

On the other hand, it was good for me because it made me go to visit a young couple living in our neighborhood. From the way they lived, I could see for the first time that they were not just Christians on Sundays, but also Christians all through the week.

What I saw in their home bore fruit. I became a Christian. This was five months ago. I recognized my sins, confessed them and know that I'm forgiven.

I really don't know how to continue—where to start and where to end. Maybe it's best to write a few of my thoughts about your book. I have worked through it two or three times and have finally come to the point where I can identify with

Ilona, even though the answers don't always apply in my case.

I masturbated (I'll use M.) for the first time when I was eleven or twelve, I believe.

Four months ago a new fellow came to our youth group. He was a real challenge to me, not as a boyfriend to go steady with, but as someone with whom I could always have a very good talk. During the time that I was seeing him, M. was never necessary.

One day through this friend I met a twenty-three-year-old, married man. When I was with him alone in my room, I again didn't know my limits. Petting! After that we saw each other twice. Petting! Petting!

Since then, M. happened four or five times, every time because my body wanted something, and I gave in to it. But what shall I do when my body longs for this quick release, especially just before my period?

The day before yesterday, I had the urge in the evening, though it did not come from my body but consciously from my mind. I read a tract about sex and that made me think it was okay to do it. So in the future I have to watch what I read.

My counselor knows nothing about all this. He and his wife are very good friends with whom I spend most of my free time. I have a very, very good girl friend who also became a Christian a short while ago, and I can talk to her about everything. . . .

This is where I stopped writing two days ago. In the meantime I had a long talk with my counselor. The Holy Spirit had told me that I should not be afraid to go to someone and say, "Pray for me. I'm in trouble."

I prayed with him and afterward I prayed alone for a long time. Most of my fears left me. I feel sheltered and at home with my Lord, just as if I could lie down, sit and walk in his hand. It's almost as if I'm not living anymore here on earth, but just in the Lord. I'm very, very happy.

I believe that M. is not necessary for me anymore. Somehow I was always looking for my place, for love and tenderness. Now

I have finally understood and feel that only God can give this, and he does.

Many thanks!

Beate

Dear Beate,

You have described a long road in your life, and I thank you for allowing me to share it and walk along with you. You are not yet in heaven, and the feeling that you don't live here on earth anymore will not last. Your way will lead through mountains and valleys, but you are going in the right direction.

Of course your situation is different from that of Ilona. She was already seventeen with no sexual experience. Your way is much harder because your sexual feelings have been aroused much too early, and you have experienced what you cannot yet digest. This was not good for you and it was not the will of God.

You must also understand the reaction of your frightened mother. She may have her faults, but she wanted to protect you from worse things and pulled the emergency brake. Of course, it would have been better if your father had entered the picture.

On the other hand, you have a great advantage in comparison to Ilona: You have a counselor who senses when you are in need and who, at the same time, has the authority to act spiritually. He can help to replace your father who left you in the lurch. I can only advise you to trust your counselor completely and tell him everything, even when you have back-slidden after your conversion. Allow him to be very strict with you and ask you direct questions.

After having gone astray for such a long time, not everything will change from one day to the other. There will still be defeats, but it is important that you confess them immediately and ask for God's forgiveness. The couple with whom you visit and your girl friend are your best helpers. Maybe even that young man who did not become a boyfriend "to go steady with," but really a friend, is also a helper.

As a further ally in your struggle you should put your intelligence to work. All you have to do is to decide never again to stay alone in a room with a man. Is that really so difficult?

There's a connection between masturbation and petting. Actually, petting is mutual masturbation. The majority of girls never discover M. Many girls are introduced to petting practices by their boyfriends. Then when the boyfriend breaks off the relationship, after having nibbled a little bit, they feel left in the lurch. Now their situation is difficult. Their sexual feelings are awakened, and so they try to find sexual pleasure without a partner, and they begin to masturbate. With some it could easily become a daily habit.

I think it is good that already you are able to discern whether you are overcome by a physical urge or whether it is a conscious, willful decision.

In any case, M. is a misuse of God's gift of sexuality. Sexuality is meant for communication, as a present to another person. If one gets stuck in M. he or she will never experience this dimension and thus deprive himself or herself of something very precious.

You've already understood a very deep mystery which many adults have not yet understood. In the final analysis, it is only God who can give you a place, who can give you love and tenderness. Praise God for this insight.

My wife and I send you our kindest greetings,
W.T.

Reflection

Since this last letter Beate has written to us often. Her letters describe her struggles, her ups and downs. Her defeats, however, are becoming more and more rare. I visited her once with her counselor. Our talk then confirmed and completed the picture of her we had formed from her letters.

Basically, the situation of Beate is the same as that of Martina and Gerda—a cold, dominating mother who gives orders and punishes rather than using the opportunity for an understanding and loving talk to guide her daughter. At the same time, they all have passive fathers who do not take a stand on the issues and who are therefore of little help to their daughters in finding their identity.

The only difference is that Beate does not seek the way out in a homosexual friendship as did Martina and Gerda. Beate believes she can replace through heterosexual activities what her parents did not give her.

This is one reason for the great misunderstanding in heterosexual friendships at this age. Usually, girls are not looking for sex but rather, as Beate has put it, "a place, love and tenderness." A boy in her peer group is not able to give this to her. He usually understands her approach as a wish for sexual activities and thinks that he is doing her a favor when he offers it to her. At first, the girl may also think she can find what she is looking for in sex. She realizes her mistake too late.

This is why those friendships which do not follow the way of Fritz and Brigitta (see chapter fifteen), but which include sex, usually end in a dead-end road. It's only a matter of time before both of them realize it. They meet on different levels and do not really find each other. Often the girl realizes this before the boy does. She may know in her heart that there is no future in their relationship, but she keeps on in order not to lose her friend.

Deep down in her heart, Beate is not looking for a boyfriend, but for a father. That's why she was most tempted by older, married men. If fathers could only understand how much they could help their daughters and protect them by consciously giving them time and attention. They could also help by showing their daughters a tenderness which does not shy away from physical expression. But many fathers are afraid of their growing daughters and withdraw in fear.

Beate is saved by her faith. Her story illustrates that true faith is not a luxury item which does not affect the basics of life, but a reality, a power which forms and changes and affects the fundamental issues of life.

In the final analysis even the best parents cannot fulfill the deepest longings of their children. Neither can a wife fulfill the longings of her husband nor a husband fulfill the deepest longings of his wife. The greatest fulfillment can only be had through a personal relationship to God. The relationship between parents and children and between husband and wife can only, in the best cases, be a mirror of this relationship to God.

If Beate has a weak father, Peter has a strong one. His letter illustrates that this fact in itself does not solve all problems.

"I'm twenty and I've never slept with a girl"
17

"As a psychiatrist, my dad is of the
opinion that premarital sex is necessary. . . .
Under the surface, my friends think that it is
a rite of manhood to seduce a girl in the
shortest possible time. . . . She said to me,
'My rule is: No lower than the waistline.' "
Peter R., age 20   girl friend, age 17

Dear Sir:

My girl friend gave me your book *Love Is a Feeling to Be Learned.* You have written the book in a way that has won my confidence. I would like to tell you that I agree with you in almost everything. Incidentally, I had come to similar conclusions the day before I read your book.

I'm twenty and I've never slept with a girl (that's a strange combination of facts in one sentence, but I can't think of a better way to put it). Most of my friends, if not all of them, have already slept with at least one girl. Under the surface, my friends think that it is a rite of manhood to seduce a girl in the shortest possible time.

Ten days ago I got acquainted with a girl. Even though we hardly knew each other, we soon realized that basically we had the same outlook on life, and so it happened that already after half an hour we talked very frankly about a lot of things. In the course of our talk she said to me, "My rule is: No lower than the waistline. Everything else belongs to marriage." (She said she was a dedicated Christian.)

You can imagine that this upset my plans. But she was so attractive I continued to go with her. In spite of our different views on sex, I fell in love with her.

I've made the firm resolution to refrain from sexual activities because the girl is too precious to me. We like each other very much—by the way she just turned seventeen—so we have already talked about marriage. And this after one week and four days!

I would like to know your opinion about this. I also talked to my father, who's fifty-six, about it. As a psychiatrist, my dad is of the opinion that premarital sex is necessary in order for the partners to see if they fit together sexually. From his experience with his patients, many marriages failed because the partners were sexually incompatible.

Please don't think that my father is an atheist. On the contrary! He believes that there would be fewer neurotics if people were oriented toward God and lived according to the rules of a religion.

Thank you very much for your interest in my problem and for deciphering my handwriting.

In respect,
Your Peter

Dear Peter!

You know, Peter, I believe you belong in a museum, not because you are old-fashioned—you may even be ahead of your time—but because a young man like yourself is so rare today. I can only congratulate you. You are simply tops!

I'm deeply impressed that you are able to resist not only peer pressure, but also the advice of your own father, given with the whole weight of his psychiatric experience.

The more I think about your letter, I dare to guess that there might be many young people—boys and girls alike—who think and feel as you do. But they are made to feel so insecure that they don't dare express what they really feel. There may be more of your friends who belong to this group than you really think. But they don't want to admit to others that they are dissatisfied. Their egos are too weak to swim against the stream—however, it's really a question of which direction the stream is running.

I believe that magazines which deal with this subject give a completely wrong picture. A young man who thinks as you do is simply not interesting for the news media. The media are interested in the others. Therefore, the impression that emerges is that all young people today sleep together as a matter of course and are very happy about it—both facts are untrue.

As far as your meeting with this girl is concerned, I think the most helpful thing was that you were able to talk together. This alone has deepened your relationship.

It is not wrong to talk about where to set the limits. On the other hand, the cut-and-dried rule about the waistline is silly. A young woman may be much more sensitive and aroused when touched on her breasts than on her genitals. You can conclude from this that sometimes it may be up to the young man to set narrower limits as the woman may overestimate her control.

If you do this then you would pass the test of being a man! After such a short time it is certainly too early to talk about marriage. On the other hand, you should be aware that for a young woman the idea of marriage is usually somewhere in the background as soon as she favors a young man.

As far as your father is concerned, you have to take into consideration that as a psychiatrist he mostly has to deal with sick people. But I don't think one can generalize this statement—saying that having intercourse together is a criterion for choosing a partner—even for healthy people. If their union is a success and they marry on this basis, they will soon see that this alone is not enough to fill their marriage with contentment that lasts a lifetime. It also often happens that people marry out of a sense of duty because they have already gone too far, even though they have a premonition that their personalities do not harmonize.

In case they have had sexual experiences with several partners, the possibility of comparing is a disadvantage when it comes to building up an exclusive and unique relationship in marriage. Research studies have shown that the divorce rate is lowest in those marriages where the partners knew no one else sexually except their spouse.

If your father had in mind the danger of a sexual neurosis, I would say that it is the result of forced repression for negative reasons, not, as in your case, a voluntary renunciation for the purpose of gaining greater maturity.

Of course, I agree with your father completely that it is psychologically healthy to be oriented toward God and to "live according to the rules of a religion." Only I see a certain contradiction between this conviction and the advice he gave you.

Did he mean by "rules of a religion" something different than the Ten Commandments of God? They are clear-cut. The expression "to become one flesh" in the Bible is exclusively related to marriage. According to biblical thinking, the state of marriage and the physical union—in this sequence—are coupled together unequivocally (Gen. 2:24).

Many claim that the Bible doesn't say anything about premarital relations. This is not true. You can read the very strict rules about premarital life in Deuteronomy 22:13-30 which in some cases even involved the death penalty.

Even in the New Testament, the alternative is unequivocal: "But if you cannot restrain your desires go ahead and marry" (1 Cor. 7:9). So it is either abstinence or marriage, but no compromise in between.

Also, the embarrassment of Joseph in view of Mary's pregnancy cannot be explained if it were not clear in the Bible that intercourse between an engaged man and woman does not correspond to the will of God (Mt. 1:18-25).

This is what I would understand by "rules of religion" in your case. But what impressed me so much in your letter was the fact that you followed these rules instinctively even though you were not conscious of them.

Continue on this road and don't allow anyone to confuse you.

I greet you cordially,
Your W.T.

Reflection

Peter's letter shows the great insecurity in our time about sexual ethics. A young man like him feels so alone that he might even doubt whether he is still "normal" if he has not yet had intercourse at the age of twenty.

I believe he belongs to a silent minority—or is it even a majority?—who live, in spite of the many sexual temptations and permissiveness of our society, in an old-fashioned, clean way following their healthy instincts. Their backbones need to be strengthened.

My children had the impression when I read the letter to them that Peter as well as his girl friend seem to think that being a Christian means to follow certain rules.

I think they are right. Neither Peter nor his girl friend know that rules and laws are not the essential issue. Being a Christian means having a personal relationship with Jesus Christ. If this relationship is established, one experiences the truth of God's promise "I will teach you the way you should go and I will lead you with my eye upon you" (Ps. 32:8). It is this personal eye contact which Peter and his girl friend have yet to experience.

This issue of a personal relationship to God and a personal relationship to a girl is the topic of the last correspondence.

"My conflict: being a Christian or having a girl friend"
18

"When I was eleven, I started to become a teen-ager. . . . I noticed that as a boy I was popular with girls. . . . The conflict is now within me—being a Christian or having a girl friend."
Rudi K., age 16, high-school student

Dear Mr. and Mrs. Trobisch,

The reason why I'm writing you at such a late—or rather early—hour is as follows. I'm sixteen and go to high school, and I am —or at least I was—a Christian.

When I was eleven I started to become a teen-ager. By this I mean I was a little bit ahead of myself. And my lifestyle changed. When I was about twelve, I fell in love for the first time. At the end of my thirteenth year, at a retreat I became a Christian.

(Excuse my handwriting—I'm in bed.)

After that I gave up all relations with girls. This was possible for me because of a very close friendship with one of my classmates.

At the end of my fourteenth year, I went to a party again for the first time. There I realized that in spite of my being a Christian, I was accepted by my classmates, including the girls.

(I'm now a little tired. It's 11:45 P.M.)

At the end of my fifteenth year, I took dancing lessons at a dance studio. I sensed that it was very easy for me to invite a girl to dance. And when it was the "ladies' choice" I was among the first ones to be asked. In short, I noticed that as a boy I was popular with girls.

It was in the middle of the dance course that a particular girl tried to win me as her friend. I was not attracted to her very much. I also thought that as a Christian I was not supposed to start a friendship with a non-Christian girl. She was very disappointed when, in spite of the fact that she was sitting beside me, I asked another girl for the next dance. Then she tried in many different ways to be able to dance with me. I don't want to describe her methods here because I wouldn't finish until tomorrow (midnight).

My problem is this: I am relatively popular with girls, and I would like to have closer contact with one girl, but all the Christian girls I know stick together in a tight group so that a closer personal relationship with one of them is impossible.

It wouldn't be difficult to get close to a non-Christian girl, but I don't think that, as a Christian, I would have a meaningful relationship with an unbelieving girl. It seems to me that either the friendship or my being a Christian would not survive. This is my thinking.

I'm sorry to say that my Christian life has gone down into a deep valley because of this unsolved problem. My personal Bible study is sort of dead, if I do it at all. The Bible doesn't speak to me anymore. I still pray and talk to God. But I'm lacking the spiritual zest I had before I started the dance course. Since that time, I have felt like I'm going downhill spiritually.

The conflict is now within me—being a Christian or having a girl friend. To my closer friends, I'm becoming untrustworthy because sometimes I feel attracted to the Christian faith and other times I am attracted by a non-Christian girl.

12:30 A.M.

Yours,

Rudi

Dear Rudi,

Thank you for your midnight letter. I see that your Christian faith means something to you and that you try to harmonize your lifestyle with your faith. This makes me very happy because there are a lot of young people who call themselves Christians but do not draw any practical consequences from this fact. I'm glad you are different.

Your best helpers are your "closer friends." You say yourself that the friendship with one of your classmates helped you the most when you tried to break with the superficial lifestyle of today's teen-agers. So this friendship pointed you into the right decision. You should cultivate and invest much time into such friendships. You will receive exactly as much confidence as you give. What happened to this friend in the meantime? With such a friend you should talk over the many small decisions you have to make when it comes to dealing with the opposite sex and examine your decisions before God.

On the other hand, I am also glad that you are not simply withdrawing but daring to stick your neck out and to meet with girls. It's also good that you are conscious of how you affect girls. Now you have to learn to deal with this in a responsible way. Evidently, God has given you an outgoing personality. This is a great gift, but you have to learn to master this gift, and you can only learn if you do not avoid being with girls.

That's why I don't think it's wrong that you took these dancing lessons, even though it led your spiritual life into a crisis. But it would be too cheap a solution to solve this crisis by withdrawal. The goal is rather to expose yourself to the head wind and in spite of it remain near to God. The only advice I would give is that you do not yet try to enter into an exclusive relationship with a girl. It is good to be acquainted with several girls at the same time and to date several without going steady with any one of them. It's only possible to make a choice if you know more than one.

However, I have the impression that you divide up the girls into Christians and non-Christians in a much too simple way. How can you know for sure? Can you look into their hearts? There may be a girl who doesn't talk much about it, but in her heart she might be in deeper fellowship with God than another one who witnesses to everyone at every occasion that she is a true believer.

Also, you have to reckon with the possibility that a girl might call herself a Christian, but this has nothing to do with her lifestyle. Recently, a sixteen-year-old girl wrote me that she prayed with her boyfriend, and afterward they went to bed together. She didn't seem to sense any contradiction.

On the other hand, there might be girls who have no idea whatsoever about Christianity, and still they have preserved a healthy instinct for what is right and a natural feeling of modesty so that they wouldn't try to lead you into temptation in any way.

You see that it is not that simple to divide them into sheep and goats. If you think of yourself in your present state, you see how difficult it would be to categorize you. I feel that as long as you keep your relationships with girls on the basis of a non-exclusive acquaintance, you don't have to be afraid. You also have to learn to deal with non-Christian girls. In later life you will be confronted again and again with non-Christians. I admit that an exclusive relationship with a girl who has no personal faith might bring you into conflict with your own faith. A mere acquaintance would not. Before you make the choice of your life partner, the question of faith will not really become decisive. Allow yourself time for this choice and accept my warm greetings.

W.T.

Dear Mr. Trobisch,

Thank you so very much for your letter. I know I should have answered it much earlier and not have waited for months. I hope you will be able to excuse my long silence.

You have not disappointed me with your answer. Step by step, I understood a little bit more of your letter. I see that grace allows one to be able to wait and to renounce certain things for one's own good.

At the moment I have good fellowship with several Christian girls, and I think I have a good relationship with each one of them. I believe that even the fact of sharing a common faith does not give one the right to start an exclusive relationship. I have made this mistake more than once before, but I know that the meaning of marriage and sexuality is much, much deeper. It is a task and a dimension which lies ahead of me still.

However, I do thank the Lord now for the space he gives me within certain limits to get to know and understand the opposite sex. I feel that when the two opposite poles are not too close together a fruitful tension and a creative energy are produced which otherwise would be lost. This, too, is a tremendous experience. . . .

You have opened a new way for me, more difficult than the old one, demanding more tenacity and strength. But in the final analysis it is the richer way, the more fulfilled way. For this I'm thankful to you.

Rudi

Epilogue

A personal letter to you:

Right now you have done something very unusual. You have read confidential letters which originally were not meant for you. I wonder whether you have really realized how much was confided in you—how much trust was invested in you?

I hope you are as thankful to these young people as I am that they granted you insight into their private mail, and in a way laid open their hearts before you.

But what will you do with this insight? What conclusions will you draw?

Maybe as you read this book, the thought came to you to seek someone to talk to outside your family. However, I would be much happier if you would try something else first.

Maybe it struck you that the parents in these letters do not play a very positive role in this book. Many of those boys and girls wrote to me precisely because they did not feel understood by their own parents. My impression is that for many the dialogue with their own parents has been destroyed or interrupted.

Have you ever had the idea that it is not only growing sons and daughters who need help, but their parents too? Have you wondered if you could help your parents as much as they could help you?

In any case, I would like to make a very practical suggestion to you: Try to get into a dialogue with your parents.

I do not mean a casual talk which happens incidentally without preparation. No, I mean a very consciously planned dialogue.

Start with the parent with whom you feel most at ease. Later on you can do it with the other parent and still later with both together. Maybe one day you could also invite your brother or sister so that a family dialogue is created. But for the beginning it might be best to start with either father or mother.

This is the way to go about it:

Ask for fifteen minutes time. Both of you sit down in comfortable chairs or on the floor. You will see that sitting on the floor gives a special feeling of fellowship and of being on the same level. Each of you needs a little notebook. You agree about a question (you will find suggestions for such questions at the end of this letter, but you could think of other questions yourself). The question should touch on something which is close to your heart.

Each of you notes the question in his or her notebook, and then you have five minutes to answer it in writing. After five minutes you exchange the notebooks and each one reads quietly what the other one has written. Then talk about it for ten minutes. Not longer. If you plan a longer time you never get around to starting in the first place.

When you talk it is important that you do not have a discussion but a dialogue. The point is not to reach an agreement or find a solution or convince the other one that you are right. The point is only to learn what the other person thinks and feels, to accept his or her opinion even if you do not agree and to accept his or her feelings even if you cannot share them.

Note: Feelings are never right or wrong. They simply exist. They just are. It takes courage to put into writing certain things which might disturb the other person, and at the same time to endure the pain without defending yourself or launching a counterattack, if you are hurt yourself. If you invest this courage the reward will be great.

To have a dialogue in this way means that you sit together and say to each other, "I trust you to such a degree that I dare to tell you the truth about myself, even if it might hurt you."

After ten minutes you get up and stop talking. Maybe at the end you agree about another question for the next day. Let things which have not yet been resolved stand as they are. They have lost their poison because they have been expressed, and therefore they can be dealt with.

Maybe you'll want to put this book on the table beside your parent's bed. It could be that they will read it. They might even decide one day to have such a dialogue with each other! Who knows what could happen!

I wish you much courage and joy for this work. It is work!

Yours,
Walter Trobisch

The following are suggested questions for your dialogue (most are taken from "Family Dialogue" by Betsy Larson in *Marriage and Family Living,* Oct. and Nov. 1977). They are intended to be basic questions which will just get you talking about feelings.

What do I like best about our family, and how does that make me feel?

How do I feel when I receive a compliment from someone in our family?

How do I feel when I receive a compliment from someone outside our family?

What is the meaning of my birthday to me? How does this make me feel?

How do I feel about having company for dinner?

How do I feel about going camping?

What is the meaning of Mom's and Dad's anniversary to me, and how does it make me feel?

What are my feelings as the new school year begins?

What are my feelings when I am asked to cut back or do without?

When do I feel closest to all of you, and how does that make me feel?

What are our (your) faults as parents, and how does that make me feel?

What are our (your) good qualities as parents, and how does that make me feel?

In what ways can your children (we) help? How does that make me feel?

What can we do to make our family life better? How does that make me feel?

How do I feel when Mom yells?

How do I feel when Dad gets mad at us?

How do I feel when Mom is sick?

How do I feel when I have to ask Dad for money? for use of the family car?

What is my best quality and how does this make me feel?

A man travels the world over in search of what he needs, and returns home to find it. —George Moore